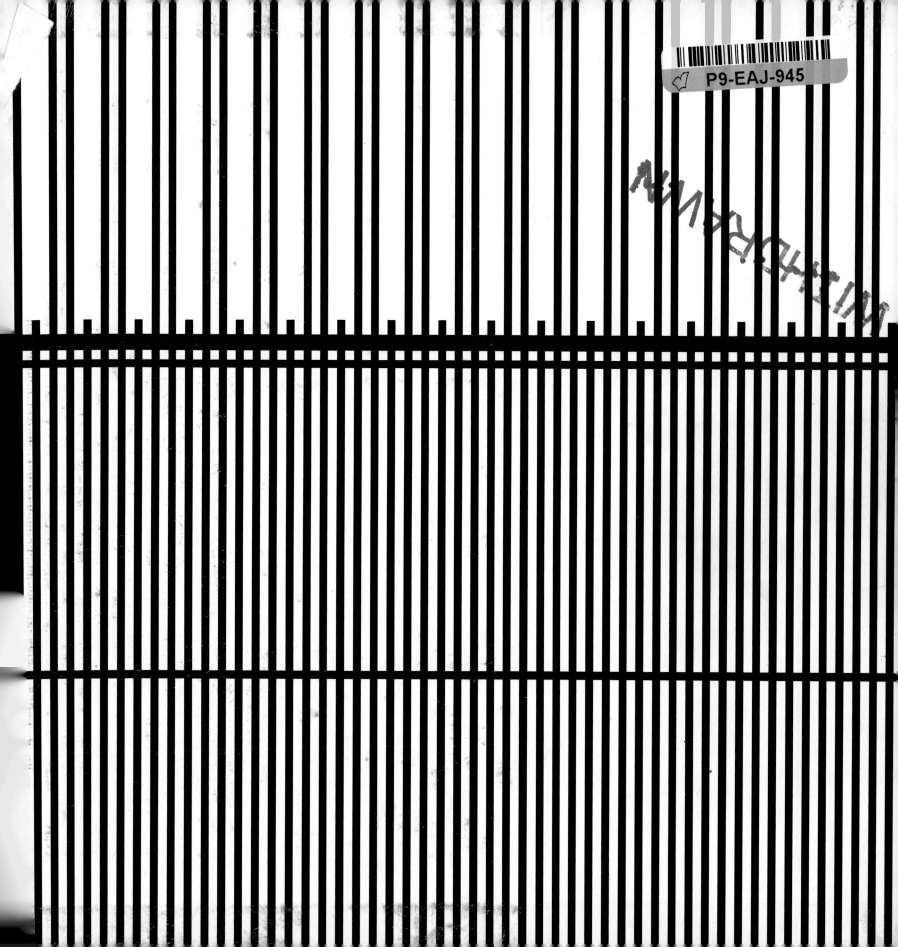

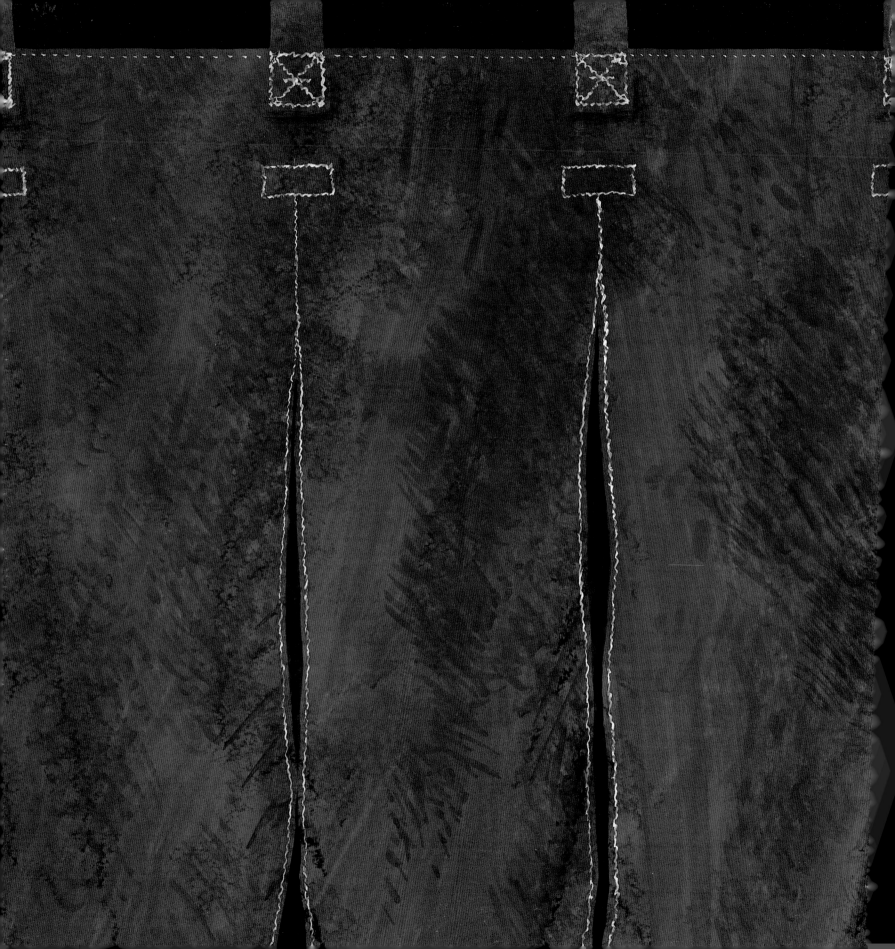

# JAPANESE STYLE

# JAPANESE STYLE

**SUZANNE SLESIN, STAFFORD CLIFF**
**& DANIEL ROZENSZTROCH**

**PHOTOGRAPHS BY GILLES DE CHABANEIX**

**DESIGN BY STAFFORD CLIFF**

**RESEARCH ASSOCIATE, KYOCHI TSUZUKI**

*Clarkson N. Potter, Inc./Publishers*
DISTRIBUTED BY CROWN PUBLISHERS, INC.  NEW YORK

TO
MICHAEL STEINBERG
JONATHAN SCOTT
PAOLA NAVONE
FRANÇOISE WINTER

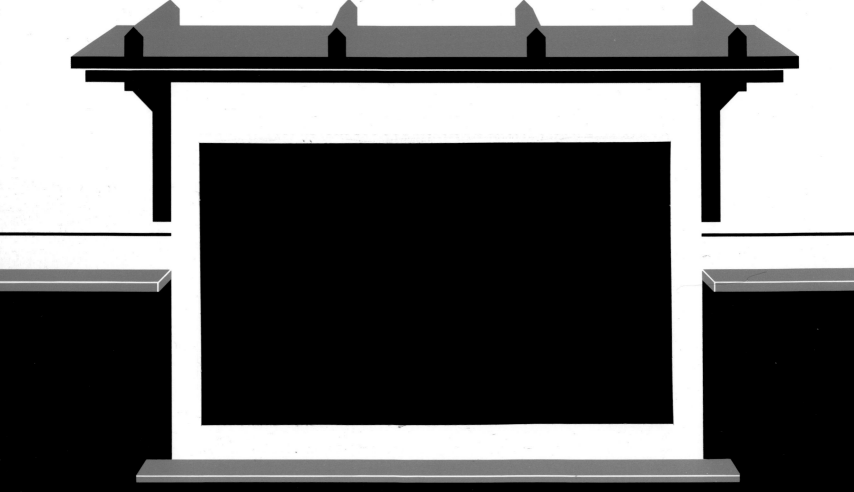

Published by Clarkson N. Potter. Inc., 225 Park Avenue
South, New York, New York 10003, and represented in
Canada by the Canadian MANDA Group

CLARKSON N. POTTER, POTTER, and colophon are
trademarks of Clarkson N. Potter, Inc.

Manufactured in Japan

Library of Congress Cataloging-in-Publication Data

Slesin, Suzanne. Japanese style.

Includes index. 1. Interior decoration – Japan – History –
20th century. 2. Interior decoration – Japan – Foreign
influences. I. Cliff, Stafford. II. Rozensztroch, Daniel. III.
de Chabaneix, Gilles. IV. Title.
NK2084. A1S64 1987          728'.0952          87-2269
ISBN 0-517-56080-1
10 9 8 7 6 5 4 3 2

# ACKNOWLEDGMENTS

We would like to thank all those who helped us find locations, offered advice and enthusiasm, translated, guided, introduced, and in general assisted us in making our way, as well as those who allowed us to photograph in their homes.

In Japan: Especially Taki Katoh, Naoko Kawamura, Teruo Kurosaki, Keizo Matsui, Kyoichi Tsuzuki. And: Tadeo Ando; Hiroyuki Arakawa; Jean-Michel, Sachiko, and Masanori Bardin; Pierre Baudry; Ina Delcourt; Nicole Depeyre; Emi Fukuzawa; Clyde Haberman; Hiroyuki Hirai; Yoshio Ineba; Reiko Ishihara; Osamu Kaivahara; Rei Kawakubo; Shinji Kohmoto; Shiro Kuramata; Masayuki Kurokawa; Itaru Maeda; Yasuo Maeda; Masakuni Matsubara; Kazu and Enne Matsushita; Mayumi Miyawaki; Seiichi and Maki Mizuno; Françoise Morechand; Masao Morikawa; Masaji Morita; Kazuko Murono; Kumiko Nagano; Kotaro Nakamura; Masato Nakayama; Taketo Oka; Setsuko Okura; Peter Popham; Kanae Rai; Makiko Sekizawa; Ryozo Shibata; Yoshihiro Shinagawa; Ikuma Sirai; Patrick Taillandier; Mutsuro Takahashi; Shizuyo Terahara; Naoko Terazaki; Philippe Terrien; Masami Togi; Ritsuko Toyama; Terry Trucco; Shigeru Uchida; Kenji Ueki; Masanori Umeda; Maxine Van-Cliffe; Ajiro and Kumiko Wakita; Kenichi Watanabe; Atsuhiro Yamada; Sumiko Yamamoto; Akiko Yanagihara; Mieko Yokoo; and Yasuo Yoshida.

In Paris: Pascal Augustin; Massakasu Bokura; Catherine, Martin, and Simon de Chabaneix; Madeleine de la Motte; Eliane Fievet; Aline Fouquet; Pascal and Myriam Herold; Marielle Hucliez; Francine Vormese; and Laboratoire Dupon.

In New York: Judith Auchincloss; Bill Bailey; Jean-Paul Beaujard; Mario Bellini; George Beylerian; Anne Campbell; Paul Casey; Lynette Cvikota; Michele Oka Doner; Yoshiko Ebihara; Laurie Eichengreen; Michael Formica; Sebastian Giefer; Joseph Giovannini; Marion Greenberg; Elizabeth Herz; Stella Ishii; J. Stewart Johnson; Jerry Kamitaki; Jun Kanai; Richard Lanier; Jack Lenor Larsen; Elaine Louie; Julia MacFarlane; Maripol, James, and Judy Miho; Ellie Rabinowitz; Paul Segal; Dora Steinberg; Joachim Beno and Lucie Rose Steinberg; Kathe Telingator; Kipp Trafton; Nob and Non Utsumi; Pilar Viladas; Mercedes Villalba; Ken Walker; Nana Watanabe; Richard Saul Wurman; and Fusayo Yakota.

In London: Andrew Cliff, Leyland Gomez, Andrew Pettit, Frank Sawkins, Maurice White, and Tsugiko Carver. Thank you also to David Kidd, who wrote the Foreword; Rosemary Levai, who compiled the Catalogue of Sources; Ian Hammond, who did all the production artwork; and Lucy Kroll, our indefatigable agent. Also to Alan Mirken, Bruce Harris, and Carol Southern, of Crown Publishers and Clarkson N. Potter, Inc., our publishers who believed in this project and supported us all along the way. We would, if we could, give a special award to our editor Nancy Novogrod, and thanks too to Jonathan Fox, Ann Cahn, Teresa Nicholas, and Laurie Stark.

Suzanne Slesin, New York

Stafford Cliff, London

Daniel Rozensztroch, Paris

Gilles de Chabaneix, Paris

February 1987

# CONTENTS

BY
DAVID
KIDD

# FOREWORD

apan today is a nation in search of a new style. A short tour of any downtown Japanese city, replete with ornate bars, discos, and "coffee" shops designed to look like, among other things, a mini-Alhambra, Tudor pub, flying saucer, or Texas ranch house, will immediately prove the point.

The rate of change in Japan is perhaps the highest in the world, turning yesterday's fantasy into still another newer and brighter Alhambra, Parisian brothel, or high-tech disco glittering in all its steel and chrome splendor.

Unlike their Chinese neighbors, the Japanese have always been curious about the world beyond their geographically isolated island shores. By necessity, they have turned the child's gift of make-believe into an art at which they excel. To live in Japan entirely bereft of one's childhood sense of play is to miss all the fun.

This art of make-believe has spilled over into the modern Japanese home, where experimentation in a thousand different styles, some of them even Japanese, is the order of the day. Make-believe is not, of course, the whole picture. Another, more serious side to Japanese nature finds its reflection in interiors that, primarily traditional in origin, have been reinterpreted in both old and new materials.

It is traditional Japan that we of the West have come most to admire, finding in its restrained art, architecture, and interiors an uncluttered elegance rare in the rest of the world. Over the centuries, the Japanese have developed a unique vocabulary of taste words to describe the quiet, unpretentious objects and interiors they have traditionally most valued.

Words like *shibui, sabi,* and *wabi* are already known in the West; indeed, whole books have been written about them, although they still defy exact interpretation. Literally they mean astringent, rustic, and lonely, yet these translations are open to endless dispute. Far better to seat oneself on the reed-matted tatami floor of a Japanese room and forget, for the moment, the barrier of words.

We will then discover that a Japanese room, composed of an astonishing number of straight lines and right angles, whatever its size, is best observed seated on the floor. From this vantage point, the lines seem to radiate from us. At the lowest level of the room, we find them in the black borders of the tatami mats, six, eight, or ten of which commonly determine the size of a room. More lines are visible in the slats of the ceiling, in the wooden latticework of the sliding doors and windows, and, most dramatically of all, in the naturally finished crossbeams and pillars of cedar, cryptomeria, and Chinese juniper composing the room's framework.

Without effort, the eye will find its way to the *tokonoma* – the alcove of honor – where an arrangement of flowers displayed in a vase calls attention to itself as the only curving lines in the room. Thus, asking no questions, we have discovered for ourselves the importance of the flower arrangement in a Japanese interior. A scroll painting hanging in the *tokonoma*, a two-panel screen opened in a corner (larger screens are used only on special occasions), an incense burner, and, in modern times only, a low table and cushions complete the furnishings.

Judging from the spartan exclusion of objects in a traditional Japanese room, we may wonder if the art of interior decorating really exists. It does, but, as we might expect, is not quite the same as in the West. In traditional Japan, the art of interior decorating depends on a heightened sensitivity to the seasons, the personality and interests of the guest of honor, and the nature of the social occasion. This implies choice – that is, the means to choose which painting will be hung, which flowers will be arranged to best suit the painting, and what receptacle will best enhance the flowers – all this to create a theme of the day, month, or season.

Setting the theme, the flower arrangement, above all, reveals the taste, education, and refinement of the householder. A wealthy family may own hundreds of flower receptacles and paintings, kept in neatly labeled boxes in a special storeroom, while any house must have at least four paintings, one for each season. As a final touch, incense – aloe, sandalwood, plum, or musk, to be burned just before the guests arrive – creates the required mood.

These few elements, multiplied by the seasons, are all that need concern the average homeowner, although on higher levels – a tea gathering, for example – rigorous connoisseurship becomes all-important. The primary decoration, the room itself, has been left to the architect, in most cases a nameless builder who followed the standards of his craft and the precepts of tradition.

In the early 1950s when I first arrived in Japan, it was customary for better Japanese homes to contain one token Western room, usually just off the entry, where the occasional guest could be entertained, without the fuss and formality required in a Japanese-style room, seated on brown overstuffed furniture arranged on a carpet in the middle of the floor around a table draped with a fringed cloth. The windows, more likely than not, were of colored glass, while at least one brown-hued oil painting, or a photograph of one, hung permanently above both the dark wainscoting and the eye level of anyone who cared to look at it. The effect created was one of an overwhelmingly brown and gloomy coziness.

Today, most of these rooms are gone, destroyed by progress in the form of a doubled population, changing taste, and rising land values, along with the buildings that once contained them. In their place, new and smaller concrete houses in the Western style, all their rooms now filled with "up-to-date" furnishings, have relegated the memory of the old house to one token Japanese room in the traditional style.

It is out of such enormous changes in the Japanese lifestyle that many contemporary interiors have emerged. We may deplore the loss of the old, but we cannot deny that this pell-mell search for the new on the part of the Japanese has brought with it an exciting glimpse of styles compatible with differing needs and a growing sense of individuality.

Modern Japanese interiors are perhaps best seen as a product of the twofold Japanese character — the playful versus the serious, the loud versus the quiet, the child as opposed to the adult, and above all the novelty of make-believe played out against the restraining weight of how-things-have-always-been. To be sure, these two aspects of Japanese character have been present throughout history, but it is only since World War II that so many Japanese have had the freedom and the money to experiment on such a grand scale.

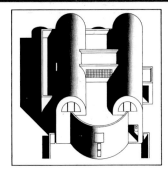

Let me end with the story of a corner — a corner of a room I first saw in Japan. The year was 1950, and I was traveling aboard the old *President Wilson* en route from Hong Kong to San Francisco. Our second port of call in Japan was Yokohama, fire-bombed like most Japanese cities, and a hodgepodge of jerry-built shacks and sheds. Some sported brave facades like nothing so much as an American frontier town. To my amazement, I found, on a stroll through a maze of postwar rubble, a gleaming, brand-new Japanese-style teahouse, and invited myself in.

The proprietress, who seemed genuinely happy to find a foreigner at her doorstep (she would be less happy today, I imagine), ushered me down a corridor to a tatami room where she left me, after much bowing, to return in due course with a cup of green tea and a plate of cakes. This time she left for good, leaving me to drink my tea and and enjoy the room alone.

Used as I was to rooms filled with furniture, both in the West and in the decaying splendor of the old mansions in Peking where I had lived for the past four years, this room seemed everything they were not. I knew, of course, from photographs what a Japanese room looked like. What I had not detected in the photographs was the perfection of detail, the smoothness of the woodwork, the luster of the lacquered *tokonoma* step, or the subtle match of the grain of the wood in the slats of the ceiling.

It was then that I looked at a corner next to the *tokonoma*, a place where the floor and two walls met. I had been looking at corners all my life without paying them much attention, and deservedly, since no corner I had ever seen prepared me for the shock the perfection of this one produced. I got up to look at it more closely,

and stood gazing down in wonder. A simple joining of three planes at right angles to one another, the corner was composed of a floor of wood polished as clean as a mirror, and two walls of smoothed clay tinted a greenish brown. (Years later I would discover that the finest walls in Japan were made from the mud found at the bottoms of long-used rice paddies.) Perfectly made, the corner was also perfectly clean. At the point where these three planes touched, not a particle of anything, leave alone dust, marred the knife-edge precision of the joinery.

This simple corner, by the laws of nature neither larger nor smaller, nor geometrically different in any way from any other corner in space and time, had nevertheless shown me that there existed in Japan, despite war and defeat, a living tradition of quality unequaled anywhere else in the world. At that moment, the certain knowledge came to me that one day I would return.

Japan has been my home now for the past 30 years, during which I have spent much time in search of the kind of beauty I found that day in a Yokohama teahouse. By now I should be accustomed to it all, yet a window opening onto a grove of bamboo in a garden, the silvery sheen of antique woodwork, or the afternoon light falling at just the right angle across the pale green of freshly laid tatami, still has the power to inspire me, as of old, with an overwhelming beauty.

*David Kidd, director emeritus of The Oomoto School of Traditional Japanese Arts, is an art collector and writer as well as an educator.*

# INTRODUCTION

Japan is a country that has long had appeal to foreigners, and modernists in the West have been greatly influenced by the traditional Japanese way of life. Simplicity, functionalism, and minimalism—three of the most important elements of Japanese design—have been appreciated, since the 19th century, and reinterpreted by Western designers and architects.

During the last decade, American and English designers and consumers have embraced the new Japanese esthetic with enthusiasm, especially in the area of industrial design—cars and stereo equipment coming first to mind. But the lifestyle of the contemporary Japanese has until now eluded their Western counterparts.

When we undertook to create *Japanese Style,* we hoped to find homes that would help us understand the living styles emerging in Japan today. All of us involved—writer, art director, stylist, and photographer—had been warned about the traditional reticence of most Japanese to invite anyone into their houses or apartments, least of all people who wanted to photograph them. In Japan, privacy is sacrosanct, and as Bernard Rudofsky wrote in *The Kimono Mind,* "solitude is a status symbol." Entertaining nearly always takes place outside the home, and requests to visit someone's living place are usually responded to with polite refusals.

Our search for stylish interiors was time-consuming but intriguing. What we were looking for were both traditional and modern homes that were somehow special—places where the occupants had made their mark, asserted their personalities.

At the outset, we obtained the help of a number of people—journalists, architects, artists, and fashion designers, as well as interpreters, marketing and advertising executives, and friends and relatives—who had the patience, perseverance, persuasiveness, and enthusiasm required to gain us entry to many of the homes we eventually photographed. Being foreign also became an advantage, as we were not so bound by the deeply instilled customs and etiquette of Japan and could make requests and inquiries that the Japanese themselves might have considered improper.

One of the surprises that was hardest to cope with was our discovery that Tokyo, a city of over 12 million inhabitants, has only about five major streets with names, and houses that, instead of being numbered sequentially according to their position on a street, are numbered according to the sequence in which they were built. And, in fact, certain suburban neighborhoods have been laid out like mazes just to discourage uninvited visitors.

Even natives of Tokyo call ahead for detailed directions to any destination and are frequently guided to a landmark such as a subway stop where they are told to wait until they can be met. The Tokyo taxi drivers were helpful as well as compassionate, refusing to abandon us unless absolutely certain that we had been delivered to the right address. Not infrequently, the driver himself would make telephone calls on our behalf, well aware of our total inability to communicate. The exhilaration we felt arriving at a destination proved to be as strong as the frustration of the hours spent searching for it.

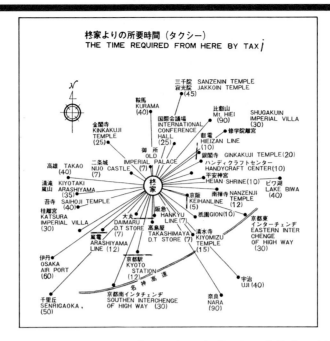

柊家よりの所要時間（タクシー）
THE TIME REQUIRED FROM HERE BY TAXI

We did not go to Japan as experts in any aspect of Oriental culture. And in a way, that left us free to observe and document a wider variety of contemporary places. Small-space living – something that the Japanese have refined to a high art – was at the top of our list. We knew that, especially in the large cities, space was at a premium, but we could not have imagined the reality of living in such diminutive homes, creating what the architect Tadeo Ando described as "a concentrated world."

We were also familiar with the tatami mat as a basic element of Japanese interiors. Measuring 90 by 180 centimeters, or about 3 by 6 feet, the tatami mat, based on the measure of a man, is used to indicate the size of a room. Advertisements in the windows of real estate agencies describe the common "two tatami mat rooms," as well as the rarer and almost palatially proportioned "20 tatami mat rooms."

Set edge to edge in preordained configurations, the straw mats are a timeless element that figures in both centuries-old and contemporary homes. They are also one reason why it is forbidden to wear shoes inside the house. "Upon these mats the people eat, sleep, and die; they represent the bed, chair, lounge, and sometimes table, combined," wrote Edward S. Morse in *Japanese Homes and Their Surroundings,* a book first published in 1886. Very early in our cold-weather visits to houses, we learned to value wool socks and what seemed to us one of Japan's most modern luxuries – heated floors. More than a custom or a design element, the tatami mat embodies the vivid ongoing relationship between the past and the present in Japan. Even totally modern and Westernized residences usually have at least one traditional tatami room for visiting relatives.

Nearly every interior we saw in Japan, with the exception of the rigorously traditional, suggested the tug-of-war between traditionalism and modernism, between the East and the West. Sometimes the conflict leads to successful syntheses, particularly in the work of such architects as Ando. His concrete buildings owe a debt to the International Style, first developed at the Bauhaus, but they also reflect the traditional Japanese sensibilities and awareness of the natural world, in which the house is considered as one with its garden, and harmony and timelessness are seen as important elements in the perception of the physical world. In Ando's houses, the continually changing qualities of daylight, the seasonal transformations of the landscape viewed through windows and doors, and the sophisticated use of poor and rough materials create an original and lyrical modern statement.

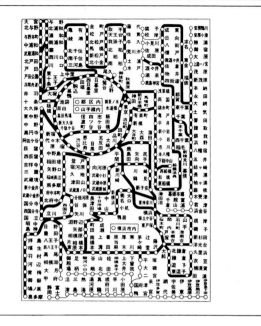

Arata Isozaki, one of the best known of Japanese modern architects and the designer of the Museum of Contemporary Art in Los Angeles, is also thought by many to be the most creative in synthesizing East and West. "As an exporter and importer of styles and ideas, Isozaki exemplifies the contemporary Japanese condition, and his career is emblematic of the play and confrontation of forces in what is still an insular country coming to grips with what it means to be international," wrote Joseph Giovannini in a *New York Times Magazine* article entitled "From Japan, A New Wave of International Architects." Isozaki, along with many of the leaders of the new generation of architects and designers — Masayuki Kurokawa, Kijo Rokkaku, Shiro Kuramata, Shin Takamatsu, Hiroshi Hara, Yasuo Yoshida, Takao Kawasaki, and Takashi Sugimoto — is wrestling with the different forces of design in Japan today. From urban housing problems to the Italian avant-garde, seemingly disparate influences are being reinterpreted and digested.

The clash between past and present, between East and West, can also generate a naive and superficial, albeit sympathetic, adoption of foreign ways. Etsuko Nakamura, a Yokohama housewife, lives with her husband, Takuo, in a modern Japanese version of the suburban American dream house. "We were living the tatami lifestyle and now we are living the chair lifestyle, and I like it much better," she was quoted as saying in the *New York Times.*

In the midst of these peculiarly Japanese responses to the traditions of the Orient and the contemporary lifestyles of the West, we also found vibrant new trends. Living in spacious recycled commercial loft buildings, designing Western-inspired furnishings from chairs to bed linens, and experimenting more freely with a wide range of industrial materials are only some examples of the directions being investigated by avant-garde and pioneering Japanese.

Along with the enthusiasm for the current and technologically up to date, we discovered in Japan — and even in Tokyo, where nearly everything is less than 50 years old — a renewed interest in time-honored values and building techniques. The crafts tradition, always strong, is being reappreciated by the modernists. While foreigners living in Japan are still drawn to the gracious rituals of the past, and the young trend setters appear to turn their backs on everything that came before, there now seems to be a strong effort toward making peace between the two attitudes — and creating what can be called the new Japanese style.

## FACES OF JAPAN

The experience of being in Japan, whether it is on a bustling neighborhood street full of Sunday shoppers or in a tranquil garden created for meditation, is always intensely visual. Flashing advertising signs overwhelm the cityscape at night; pastel candies and meticulously selected vegetables are displayed and packaged like rare jewels; a fish market, with its variety of colors and forms, becomes an esthetic experience; and the innumerable small restaurants and shops appear to spill out into the street.

All of these images are animated by the seemingly ceaseless energy of the people themselves – from kimono-clad women to blue-suited businessmen, from white-gloved taxi drivers to traditionally dressed farm workers who look as if they have stepped out of a 19th-century wood-block print.

*Far Left and Left: Seasonal splendors, from spring cherry blossoms to spectacular fall foliage, are recalled indoors by the symbolic choice of a single natural element.*

*Right:* In the Imperial Palace complex in Kyoto, the shishinden – the residence of the head of the royal household and the building used for special celebrations – features wide ceremonial steps that face the entrance gate. Rebuilt at the end of the 18th century, the spacious and strikingly designed structure is of unpainted wood, with black and dark red detailing. A series of shutters and sliding panels that open to the exterior take advantage of the large gravel-covered courtyard.

*Right:* The flashing lights and bright neon advertisements that are typical of some areas of Tokyo by night appear to contradict the image many Westerners have of Japanese restraint.

*Left:* During the day, the buildings have a quieter look and seem to be stacked up next to one another like children's building blocks.

*Left:* Serene views of the ocean and lake are in contrast to the intensely crowded cityscape.

*Right:* Learning to tee off on one of Tokyo's multidecker golf driving ranges, flying festive kites in the hills, walking along autumn leaf-strewn paths, or visiting the granite landscape at the Sogetsu Art Center, with a plaza garden by Isamu Noguchi, are some of the varied pleasures of the Japanese city and countryside.

*Left:* Crowds of people, including sweatshirted teenagers, are a common sight in Tokyo, where Sunday morning shopping along some of the popular back streets is a favorite activity.

*Right:* Snapshots of everyday Japanese life: bicyclists stopping to admire cherry blossoms in the spring; people being entertained by punk rock groups at Yoyogi Park; shoppers along a suburban paper lantern-garlanded street or in a city arcade; sweets and shoes vying for space in a Tokyo alleyway; a nighttime carnival under the cherry blossoms; schoolchildren and visitors to the Kyoto Zen garden; parents and children on a weekend outing.

*Right:* In a city like Tokyo, where the taxi drivers always wear white gloves and sometimes white caps, observing people can be as educational as it is entertaining. Telephone repairmen, a Sunday asphalt golfer, an urban fisherman, bicyclists, a stern policeman, a leather-jacketed punk rocker, a shopkeeper, baseball players, festival celebrants, and neighborhood children all contribute to the varied fabric of the city.

*Far Left: Boldly patterned* noren — *half curtains — announce a fast-food* yakitori *stand,* where broiled chicken on skewers is sold.

*Left: A clerk waits on customers at a pristine pastry shop.*

*Below Far Left: Players try their hand at Pachinko in one of Tokyo's many game parlors.*

*Below Left: Tickets for Tokyo's subway can be purchased from machines in the stations.*

*Bottom Far Left and Bottom Left: The stark, sleek, and minimal shop front of a Tokyo modern fashion boutique contrasts with the hodgepodge graphics of public telephones set next to vending machines.*

*Right: A greenhouselike variety of exotic flowers and branches fills a flower store in Tokyo.*

*Below Right: The local broom maker working in his housewares shop conveys a timeless and peaceful quality.*

*Left:* A calligrapher reads the newspaper while he awaits customers in his shop. Examples of his craft hang like banners from the ceiling or are clipped onto the crowded shelves.

*Right:* Handmade brushes, gleaming chef's knives, neat balls of twine, plastic-wrapped calculators, assortments of beans and crackers, and stacks of packaged chopsticks at every price are some of the products that are available in mind-boggling variety from Tokyo shops.

*Left and Right:* Dry candies called higashi *and* namagashi, *made of sugar, millet jelly, soy, and barley powder paste, are molded or baked into a variety of shapes. Some symbolize the seasons — flowers or cherry blossoms for spring, maple leaves for fall — while others are realistic and surprising interpretations of seemingly out-of-context foods as clams. The sweets are usually served at tea ceremonies or celebrations. And the packaging itself is important, whether it is of finely woven bamboo or a luminous piece of cellophane.*

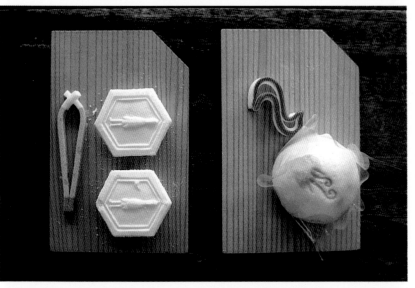

*Top and Top Right, Opposite Top Right and Top Far Right: Tokyo's Tsukiji market, one of the important marketplaces of the world, includes over 1,000 vendors. Fish and seafood – fresh, dried, and frozen – are of the best quality. Shrimp and squid, as well as whole tuna, are displayed in stalls at dawn in the glass-topped warehouse buildings.*

***Above** and **Above Right:** At the outdoor street market, merchants sell their wares, everything from cooking oil to china.*

*Above Left and Above:* Grains and beans are sold by one shopkeeper; another specializes in seaweed and other green adornments for sushi and sashimi.

*Far Left and Left:* Workers and shoppers breakfast at two of the many small curbside restaurants that offer noodle-filled soups or Western-style coffee and pastries.

*Left:* Day-glo-hued blossoms, from shocking pink to deep purple, are neatly arranged in white boxes.

*Right:* A bunch of scallions is securely tied to the back of a bicycle for delivery to a customer.

***Above and Above Right:*** *Whether exotic or ordinary, vegetables available at Tokyo markets – such as scallions, white radishes, onions, ginger root, and fiddlehead ferns – are sold in formal and esthetically pleasing packages. Looking more like festively wrapped gifts than everyday comestibles,*

*the produce is expertly arranged against crisp white paper or in wooden or plastic boxes, and, with the addition of ordinary rubber bands or even bright purple ties, these delectably fresh vegetables become artful statements.*

27

*Left and Right:* Walls and fences, as well as such varied surfaces as a bed of red autumn leaves from a Japanese maple, blossoms strewn on a garden of moss, glazed ceramic roof tile, raked gravel, tied bamboo, and smooth cement, are some of the visual textures of the landscape.

**Left:** *The rock garden at the Ryoanji temple in Kyoto, created at the beginning of the 16th century, is considered the most beautiful stone garden in Japan. The large rocks are like islands in a sea of gravel, laid out in ripplelike concentric circles. The simplicity and perfection of the landscape is the outstanding visual example of the Zen philosophy.*

# THREE DIRECTIONS

In Japan, perhaps more than in any other country, the different attitudes of the designers of houses are summarized by their choice of materials. The traditional Japanese *minka,* or folk house, with its rough exposed beams of kiaki wood often tied with rope, its thatch roof and tatami mat-covered floors, remains a powerful emblem of life around the family hearth. By contrast, the contemporary house in Japan, sometimes poetic, sometimes forbidding, and often bunkerlike in its use of concrete, stainless steel, and ceramic tile, reflects a more recent view of the house as a bulwark against the densely populated industrial city. And with prefabricated high-tech materials such as wire glass, cyclone fencing, and corrugated iron, the newest generation of young architects is creating houses that are bolder in shape, freer in spirit, and, in the way they embrace the urban environment, more independent from the values of the past.

*Far Left and Left:* A contrast in sensibilities between the old and the new is reflected in materials: stone, sisal, and polished wood, representing the old; corrugated steel, glass, and ceramic tile, symbols of the new.

*Right and Far Right:* Architect Tadeo Ando used concrete as the basic material for the design of a house near Kobe. The residence, part of which is set underground, is meant to be unified with the natural world around it. Architectural spaces and surfaces appear to change constantly as the sunlight is reflected on walls, steps, and roofs.

## MODERN RESIDENCE

Tadeo Ando is one of Japan's foremost architects, and his work, especially his residential projects, epitomizes the translation of traditional Japanese design concepts into a modern idiom. In Ando's reinterpretation of the Japanese house and its garden, views of grass, bushes, and trees are replaced by the play of light and shadow. The architect manipulates natural light in order to create a constant sense of the natural world as it changes and affects both the exterior and interior spaces of the house.

Ando's 1981 house designed for the fashion designer Hiroko Koshino is a multilevel building set on a hilly site near Kobe. Instead of wood, the traditional building material of Japan, the structure is made of concrete. Inside, the bare walls act as canvases for the evolving light patterns. The rooms, connected by corridors, are designed to take advantage of the rhythmic reflections of light and shade within the interior. Other surfaces are of natural materials meant to change with age – grass matting on the floors, cotton upholstery, and wood tables and cabinetry – creating a sensual contrast with the concrete.

*Far Left: Steps lead down to the front door of the house, which is inset in a glass wall.*

*Left: Light creates a rhythmic pattern through long thin windows in the hall that line the bedroom wing.*

*Right: The play of shadow and light on an exterior wall forms a strong graphic composition.*

*Above and Right:* The high-ceilinged living room is situated at the end of a narrow passage. Openings at the top of the walls allow some light to enter while keeping the room rather dark.

**Above:** *The cotton-upholstered Western-style furniture is low and comfortable. Floors are covered in sisal matting. One of the only strong colors in the space is provided by the red-lacquered coffee table.*

**Left:** *Large expanses of glass frame the view from the living room to the exterior.*

*Top:* The end of the long wood dining table is cantilevered over the living room.

*Above:* The staircase, dining room furniture, and kitchen cabinets are all made of wood – a material meant to be pleasant to the touch.

*Above:* The kitchen counters and appliances are of stainless steel. Western-style chairs surround the dining table.

**Above:** *A large piece of pottery sits at the bottom of the steps outside the dining room.*

**Left:** *Part of Hiroko Koshino's collection of antique Oriental china is stacked up on a serving counter in the dining area.*

**Top:** The master bedroom is located slightly below ground level for visual privacy.

**Above:** The desk and headboard are made of smoothly intersecting wood planes.

**Left:** Books and magazines line the bare wall in the master bedroom. Light enters through a slot in the ceiling.

*Right:* One of the terraces overlooks the countryside.

*Below Right:* The peaked thatched roof is typical of old folk houses.

## TRADITIONAL JAPANESE FARMHOUSE

The peaked and thatched roof, rope-tied beams, and centrally placed fireplace are all typical characteristics of the traditional Japanese farmhouse built about two and a half centuries ago. No nails were used in the construction of the folk houses, or *minkas,* which were made for the most part with wood from the indigenous kiaki tree.

In the last decade, many such farmhouses from the more rural parts of the country have been taken apart to be reassembled and outfitted with modern conveniences – new kitchens and glass windows, for example. Yoshihiro Takashita, an antiques dealer, and his wife, Reiko, live in a rebuilt farmhouse in Kamakura, a resort town south of Tokyo. The house not only provides the couple with an unusually spacious place to live but also functions as a background for the Takashitas' antiques.

*Right:* A chest for storing shoes is in the entrance foyer.

44

*Right:* The living room with its exposed wood beams contains a mixture of English colonial-style pieces and Japanese antiques.

*Above and Right:* A collection of blue-and-white porcelain is displayed in a cabinet and on a Korean chest.

**Above:** *Wood-and-rope clogs are used for going out to the garden.*

**Left:** *In the bathroom, there is a traditional wooden-lidded tub.*

*Right and Below Right:* The tea-ceremony room has a wall of translucent rice-paper panels and a floor covered in tatami mats.

*Far Right:* A spectacular antique porcelain bowl is set out on a table near the window.

**Above and Above Right:** *Antique baskets used for flower arrangements are displayed in the small sitting room under the eaves.*

**Left:** *Western-style Oriental chairs and a low lacquered table are part of the furnishings in the sitting room.*

**Left:** *The beams of the house are held together with rope.*

**Below Far Left:** *A collection of unusual 19th-century wicker baskets is grouped on a low table.*

**Below Left:** *The textured walls are of wood that has been painted.*

**Right:** *An enormous piece of pottery stands under the thatched roof in the attic room.*

*Right, Below Right, and Far Right: Sited on steep terrain, the house has a perforated-steel geodesic dome that gives it a gymnasiumlike look.*

## AVANT-GARDE ENVIRONMENT

Choosing prefabricated industrial elements over reinforced cement, and embracing the urban landscape instead of trying to deny it, are basic themes in the work of Toyo Itoh, one of the leading young architects of the postwar generation in Japan.

Itoh lives in Tokyo with his wife, Ritsuko, the program director at NHK TV, a leading network, in an open, light-filled house of his own design. All the high-tech materials – sheets of aluminum, perforated steel panels, and canvas – are of standard sizes. They are combined to create an innovative environment, which extends the vocabulary of Japanese modernism.

*Above and Far Right:* The courtyard, partially covered in canvas, acts as an open-air living room. All the rooms are connected to the main space.

*Right:* See-through metal was the material chosen for the door to the courtyard.

*Above:* The metal ceiling is a surprising element in the traditional tatami room.

*Top Right:* In the kitchen a long freestanding counter contains the sink.

*Above Right and Right:* Teruaki Oohashi designed the geometric furniture in the barrel-vaulted living space.

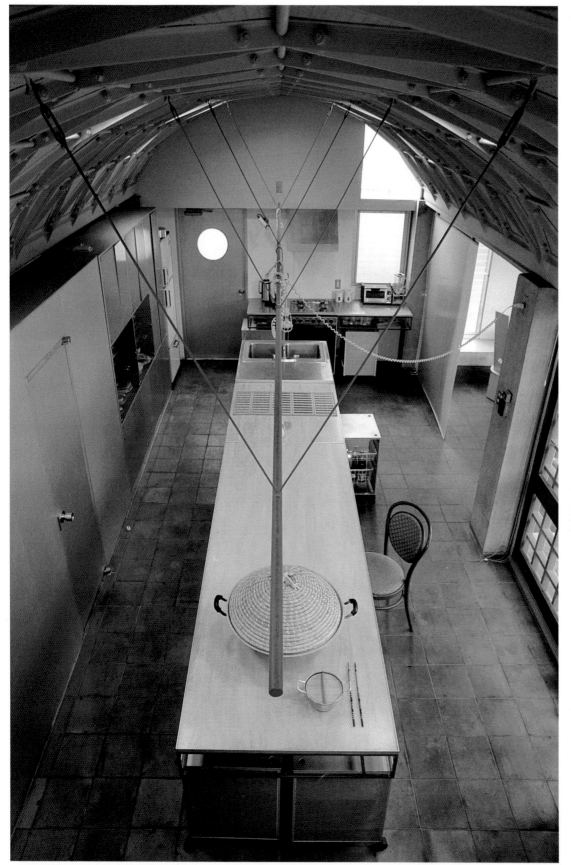

**Above:** *An opening in the roof lets light into the kitchen.*

**Left and Top:** *The counter stretches the length of the kitchen. Small units on wheels provide storage underneath.*

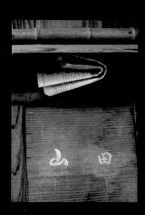

## LOOKING EAST

Conserving the mores of the past is an essential part of modern Japanese life. Taking off one's shoes before going indoors remains a universal Japanese practice. Ritual baths, futons for sleeping, low tables for eating, and tatami-covered floors for sitting also speak of the endurance of traditions.

The privacy of the home is maintained no matter what its size. Although the television set is becoming an ubiquitous presence, many houses are devoid of the myriad decorative possessions that fill Western interiors. There is little space or need for entertaining on a large scale. Usually, the Japanese interior is restrained and orderly, and in the way that it recalls the calm and peacefulness of the past, it has become a modern classic in its own right.

*Far Left and Left: A contemporary tea-ceremony room by modern architect Tadeo Ando continues the woodcrafting techniques seen in the details of ancient houses.*

## HILLSIDE MANSION

David Kidd, a writer, teacher, art collector, and director of a school that instructs foreigners in the traditional arts of Japan, left the United States when he was 19 years old and lived for many years in China before moving to Japan 30 years ago.

For the past seven years, Kidd has resided in an old house on a hillside in Kyoto overlooking the Higashiyama, the Eastern Mountains. Built about 150 years ago, the large structure was moved to its present site in 1926. But instead of decorating it in the traditional and minimal Japanese manner, Kidd's intent was to suggest the style of an old Chinese mansion. To this effect, he has furnished the house with museum-quality Chinese antiques, including his collection of spirit stones, one of the largest in the world.

*Top Left:* The 150-year-old house is surrounded by a small garden.

*Left:* Some of the rooms look onto an interior courtyard.

*Below Left:* The siting of the house allows for a view of Kyoto in the distance.

*Right:* A heavy stone lantern stands at the end of the garden, which was created in the 1920s.

**Far Left:** *The cut-glass bowl on a rosewood stand has been placed in front of a decorative window.*

**Left:** *Seventeenth-century Chinese vases sit on two 17th-century tables that look as if they were made in the same shop.*

**Below Far Left:** *A variety of objects, including a large brush that a scholar would use for calligraphy, are displayed in a 17th-century Chinese vase.*

**Below Left:** *Scrolls are kept in a Korean Li dynasty celadon vase, also from the 17th century.*

*Right and Below Right:* In one of the house's two sitting rooms, David Kidd tried to create a balanced scheme in the Chinese manner. A pair of 14th-century black lacquer cabinets flank two 17th-century Chinese palace tables. By the window is a kang, or Chinese couch.

**Above:** *Part of David Kidd's collection of Chinese spirit stones is displayed in front of the window in the large sitting room.*

**Left:** *Reference books on Japanese, Chinese, and Tibetan art are stored in the back hall of the house, which has been converted into a library.*

**Left:** *The main sitting room has three sides of glass that overlook the surrounding garden. Dark-blue felt covers the floor, on which are scattered a number of antique Chinese carpets.*

## PLANTATION HOME

The series of connected structures, originally built about 1835 at the center of an important rice plantation, was recently declared a National Treasure. Two sisters-in-law, Tokiko and Ritsu Isa, lived in the house in the village of Yahata, outside Kyoto, until they were relocated to a small residence on the property to allow for the restoration of the historic complex.

*Left: Tokiko and Ritsu Isa stand on the gallery of the historic house.*

*Right: A covered walkway connects the different structures.*

*Far Right: The roofs of the main house are made of thatch or glazed ceramic tile.*

*Below Right: The gallery around the main house is completely open to the garden.*

*Below Far Right: Living quarters for the workers as well as storage space for rice and other crops were in adjacent structures.*

*Right:* The entrance to the estate is behind a red-walled gateway.

*Below Right:* Sliding panels allow for flexibility in the gracious suite of living spaces.

*Left: Made entirely of wood, the large kitchen has remained the same for over 100 years. It includes a floor of pavement stones and troughlike sinks.*

## GEISHA HOUSE

Miyo Nakahata lives in a 100-year-old geisha house in the Higashiyama section of Kyoto. With its facade directly on the street and its second floor shielded by thin bamboo blinds, the structure is typical of the kind of urban house still used by geishas in the aristocratic city.

A half-hidden entrance on one side of the house leads to an enclosed courtyard. The materials of the interior — well-worn stone floors, patinaed wood stairs, and yellowed rice-paper panels — are reminders of an intriguing history.

*Above:* In the evening, a geisha walks toward the house.

*Left:* A geisha in ceremonial makeup and traditional dress poses in the courtyard.

*Above:* Bamboo shades and sliding panels provide privacy from the street.

*Right and Below Right:* The small inner courtyard and garden is paved with stones.

*Far Left: On the second floor, the reception rooms are off an angled corridor.*

*Left: Each of the rooms leads onto a gallery.*

*Below Far Left and Below Left: The kitchen — with its tall bamboo cupboards, freestanding screens, stone floors, and carved stone sink — has not changed in decades. Pots and bowls are stored above the sink.*

*Right: The spacious tatami mat-covered reception room is one of many in the house.*

*Below Right: A centrally placed staircase leads to the second-floor landing by the reception rooms.*

*Below Far Right: The vintage bathroom has a shallow pale blue and white ceramic-tiled sink and a white antique ceramic tile surround edged with bamboo.*

## COLORFUL INTERIOR

Nicole Depeyre's father was a French career diplomat in Asia, and although she traveled widely, she always yearned to return to Japan, where she was born. For the last 26 years, Depeyre has been the director of Dior Perfumes in the Orient. Her traditional house in the center of Tokyo is rare for having survived from when it was built in 1939 to the present.

Depeyre furnished the two-story wooden building with only a few pieces of French furniture and a Western-style bed that hint at her European past. But it is the vibrantly colored objects she has collected from all over the Orient that act as a counterpoint to the understated, monochromatic, and minimal Japanese house.

*Left: The 45-year-old two-story wooden house is hidden behind a bamboo gate in a charming overgrown garden.*

*Right: Orchids lie on the rim of a stone basin by the house.*

*Left:* Antique porcelain Chinese ink boxes are grouped around a Buddha in the ground-floor reception room.

*Right:* The top of the small French antique desk is covered with ivory heads and boxes.

*Center Right:* Bamboo is used to support the roof tiles on the ceiling of the second-floor gallery.

*Far Right:* Pillows made from antique mandarin robes are piled up on the Thai Buddhist chair in the bedroom.

*Below Right and Below Far Right:* The sliding panels are detailed with different patterns and colors of rice paper.

*Below Center Right:* Antique Chinese runners have been laid on top of the lilac-colored carpeting in the gallery.

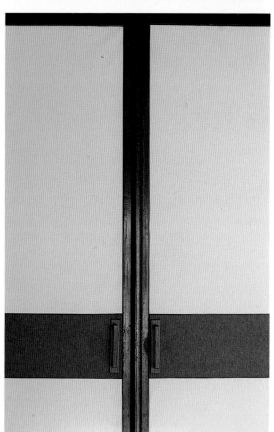

*Above:* A marriage kimono with a bright-orange crane motif, which was traditionally worn over a white kimono, is displayed in the bedroom.

*Above:* The silk panel representing a Buddha that hangs over the bed dates from the Kamakura period.

*Right:* Small decorative Chinese rugs, an antique ceremonial kimono, and a bedcover made from two vintage Japanese obis contribute to the vibrancy and feminine mood of the bedroom.

# MODEL HOME

The small house on a corner in the centrally located Yoyogi section of Tokyo is a model of middle-class Japanese life. It is the home of Renkei Kuwahara, a journalist, and his wife, Nobuko. The couple had decided to tear down the existing structure on the site and build a new house.

The simple wooden residence, designed by Naoko Hirakura, incorporates tatami mats, sliding shoji screens, and futons within a contemporary framework.

*Far Left:* The garage of the wooden house has been constructed as part of the concrete base.

*Above Center Left:* The house is reflected in a concave mirror.

*Above Left:* The letter box and doorbell are set into the gray metallic-painted wall.

*Far Left and Below Far Left:* A gallery overhangs the small courtyard, where one side is open to a tiny garden.

*Left:* The house is dwarfed by skyscrapers in the neighborhood.

*Above Right:* During the day the futon is kept out of sight in the master bedroom. A row of chests provides storage.

*Right:* The combination dining and living room is adjacent to the entrance hall.

*Above:* The narrow entrance hallway is lined with cabinets.

*Right:* In the guest room, the futon is made up for the night.

*Below Right:* The book-filled office is where Renkei Kuwahara works.

**Above:** *An old-fashioned wooden tub has been installed in the new ceramic-tiled bathroom.*

**Left:** *Personal objects are assembled on top of a chest in one of the bedrooms.*

**Below Left:** *Porcelains stored in beribboned wooden boxes are kept in the office.*

## FOLK HOUSE WITH THATCH ROOF

The farmhouse in the ancient village of Osumi, near Kyoto and Nara, has been in the same family since it was constructed in the mid-18th century. A peaked, thatched-roof folk house, it is presently the home of Kimio Sawai, a doctor, and his wife, Mieko.

The monumentally proportioned rooms are filled with family mementos and furnishings that have been handed down through the generations.

*Far Left and Center Left:* An imposing gateway marks the entrance to the house.

*Above Left:* The main entrance is under a glazed-tile overhang.

*Far Left, Center Left, and Left:* Large ceramic pots are interspersed throughout the garden.

*Below Far Left, Below Center Left, and Below Left:* Along the wide gallery surrounding the house, bamboo blinds provide shade and sliding panels open onto the interior.

*Right:* The antique rice-paper panel depicting a landscape separates the living room from the foyer.

*Right:* The six-panel antique screen, one of a pair, depicts six months of the year and is changed according to the season.

*Above:* A scene of puppies playing has been painted on a natural-wood panel in the entrance foyer.

**Right:** *Leaves inset between two thicknesses of rice paper strengthen the door-pull panel.*

**Above:** *A stone brazier sits conveniently beside the dining table in the main living space.*

**Left:** *The cupboard in the tea-ceremony room encloses small upright chests, open shelves, and a unit with sliding doors.*

**Right and Far Right:** *Wood sculptures of fish fill the clerestory openings above the sliding panels.*

**Center Right:** *A chest with porcelain boxes stands in the entrance foyer.*

**Below Right and Below Far Right:** *Framed mementos and calligraphy are hung at an angle above the doorway.*

**Below Center Right:** *Sticks of charcoal are inserted into the ashes of the floor-level brazier.*

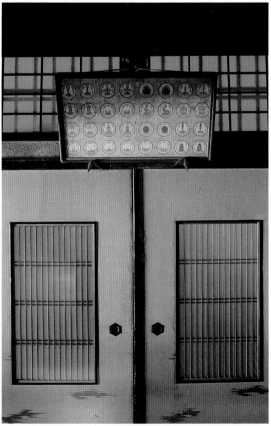

## URBAN HAVEN

From the outside, the reinforced-concrete house that belongs to Toshiaki Chine, an advertising executive, has the look of a vertical bunker. Designed by Kenji Hongo, the building with a windowless facade on a Tokyo street is meant to provide a haven insulated from the busy urban surroundings.

Inside, Chine reinterprets Oriental culture with sophisticated elements that reflect the natural world. Handcrafted materials and objects are striking contrasts to the emphatically modernistic exterior of the house.

*Left and Far Left: The five-story concrete house has no windows on the street side.*

*Below Left: Tsuneo Taniguchi created a sculpture of the owner's name for the entrance.*

*Right and Below Right: Behind the closed facade, the different floors open onto a narrow atrium that rises from the ground-floor parking space to the roof.*

*Left:* An arrangement of flowers rests on the floor of the small entrance foyer.

*Below Left:* On the top floor, a gold-hued painting by Toshimitsu Imai hangs on the wall near the large low dining table.

*Right:* A television set is stored in a custom-made unit that hides an American efficiency kitchen.

**Above:** Sliding rice-paper panels in the tea-ceremony room are decorated with a pattern of crisscrossed lines that are meant to symbolize rain.

**Right:** A small stair with an angular metal banister links the interior floors.

**Far Right:** One of the boxes that hold ritual objects for the tea ceremony sits in front of a panel of handmade paper.

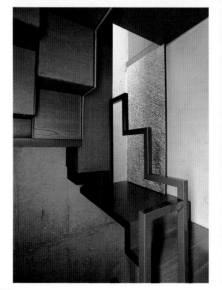

**Far Left:** *The sliding panel that doubles as a door to the tea-ceremony room is covered with another handmade paper. A modern light fixture illuminates the corridor.*

**Left:** *The unusual black tatami mats in the tea-ceremony room were inspired by the Edo period.*

**Above:** *The back wall of the tea-ceremony room is covered with paper made by a craftsman.*

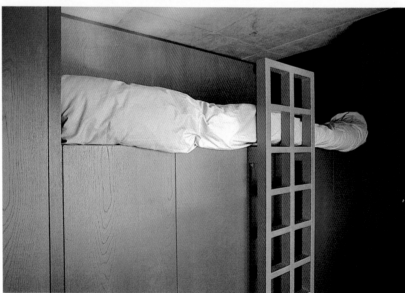

*Above:* On the interior terrace that overlooks the atrium, pottery made by contemporary Japanese artists contrasts with a modern Italian lamp and chair.

*Above:* A graphic pink ladder is used to reach the bunk bed in one of the children's rooms.

*Right:* Sunlight creates a dramatic pattern on the wall of the atrium.

## EXTRAORDINARY GARDEN

Although it was built only about five years ago, the house designed by Kazayuki Nimura for Masaji and Tomie Morita looks surprisingly old. Situated in Yamashina-ku, a residential section of Kyoto, the typically traditional residence is surrounded by an extraordinary garden that includes a pond stocked with priceless carp.

*Above:* A thick stone step is at the entrance to the courtyard.

*Far Left:* The back garden is delineated by a thatch-and-bamboo fence.

*Left:* Flat round steppingstones create a graphic pattern. Shoes to be worn in the garden are conveniently kept on the large stone near the door.

*Far Left:* In the rock garden, water runs out of a traditional bamboo spout.

*Above Right:* The path crossing the courtyard is paved with different inlaid stones.

*Right:* The tea-ceremony room opens directly onto the exterior.

**Left:** *Water flows over rocks in a color-filled corner of the garden.*

**Below Left:** *A rock is nestled in a sculptural tuft of grass.*

**Right:** *The focus of the elegant garden is a pond filled with variegated carp.*

**Above:** *A two-panel screen helps define the space in the stark entrance hall.*

**Right:** *Each element of the house, from the building materials and the colors and textures to the relations of small and large spaces and the subtle arrangement of ordinary objects, has been carefully considered so that every view is pleasurable.*

## INSPIRED BY THE PAST

The house in Kurakuen, a small town near Osaka and Kobe, was designed by the architect Kan Izue for Takamasa and Reiko Akai and their three children. The family had previously lived in a contemporary apartment and had decided they wanted to embrace a more traditional way of life. The Osaka architect is well known for integrating modern construction techniques in residences based on historical Japanese forms.

Although constructed from new materials – in this case, concrete and stainless steel – the house has a classic Japanese layout, with all rooms opening onto the exterior and garden. The roofs are lined with glazed tiles, and many of the decorative elements are inspired by antique motifs. But the electronically operated garage – spacious enough for three American cars – is a reminder of the present.

*Left and Right: The electronically controlled garage is the most futuristic element of the house. Stainless-steel doors contrast with the cobblestone driveway and roof overhang covered in glazed tiles.*

*Left:* A wide formal staircase leads up to the front entrance of the house.

*Below Left:* Glazed ceramic tiles are laid in a decorative pattern in the garden.

*Right:* The front door is under a covered porch.

*Center Right:* A stylized butterfly is made of glazed tiles set on their sides.

*Far Right:* Tiles also decorate the tops of the posts that frame the stairs leading to one of the side entrances.

*Below Right:* Glass walls are on either side of the front door. A shiny geometric pattern has been laid over the matte black floor.

*Below Center Right:* A series of flat steppingstones in the garden can be seen from one of the living rooms.

*Below Far Right:* Near the front steps, a pine tree stands in a planter edged in tile.

*Far Left: Etched glass doors with yellow frames lead to the small living room.*

*Left: The dining room is focused on the 19th-century Chinese screen, a family heirloom.*

*Below: A sliding Mondrianesque panel separates the living room from the dining room.*

*Right:* The slatted wood ceiling is one of the custom-made elements of the interior.

*Below:* Tatami mats and a black wood table furnish the tea-ceremony room.

## SPACIOUS WOOD BUILDING

In the 1950s, film director Shozo Makino lived in the huge Kyoto house that dates from the first quarter of the century. Now it is the home of Fumiko Ohta, a dancer who directs a traditional Japanese dance company, and her mother and daughter.

The two floors of the house are linked by a wide staircase, and a luxuriant and well-established garden surrounds the unusually spacious wooden structure.

*Far Left and Below Far Left: The house is set in a garden of tall trees and bushes.*

*Left: A small courtyard shields the entrance from the street.*

*Below Left: In the back, a bamboo gate leads to the garden.*

*Right: A bamboo cupboard is used for storing shoes inside the front door.*

113

*Right:* A glass-paneled corridor offers a serene view of the interior rock garden.

*Above:* One of the sitting rooms opens directly onto the garden.

*Left:* An antique Chinese table and matching stools are in the sitting room.

*Left:* The shoji screen-lined living room is occasionally used for the tea ceremony.

*Above:* Vases and lacquerware are among the objects displayed in one of the smaller sitting rooms.

*Right:* A warrior's costume and two antique chests are at one end of the sitting room.

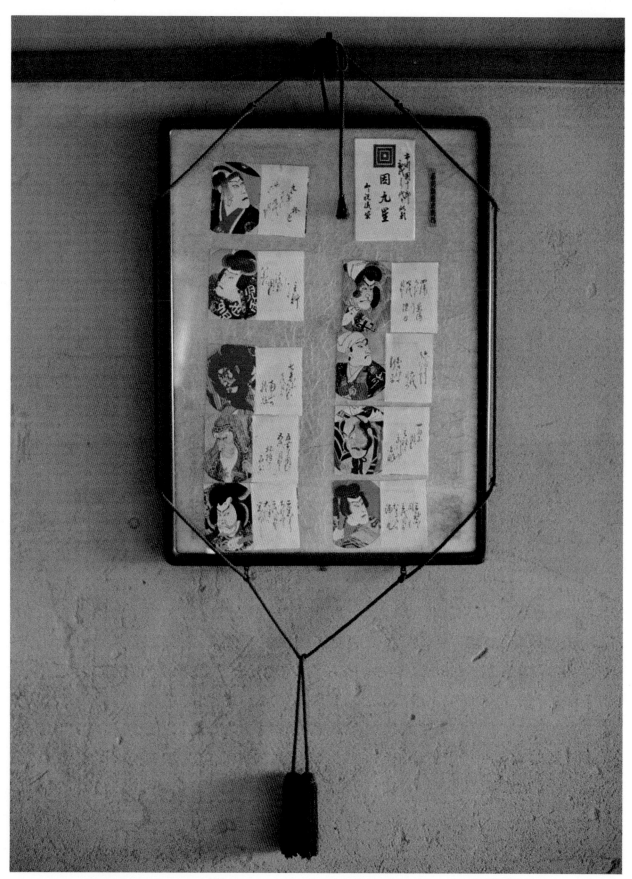

*Right:* On the second floor, sliding panels allow easy access to a covered gallery.

*Far Right:* Bowls and teapots are kept in the tea-ceremony kitchen.

*Below Right:* The bathroom features a deep wooden tub.

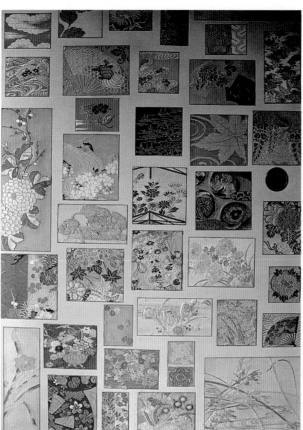

**Far Left:** *A steep stair leads to the second-floor gallery.*

**Left:** *Swatches of antique fabric create a collagelike effect on the panel-covered walls of the grandmother's bedroom.*

**Below Left:** *The electric radiator, vacuum jug, and television set are modern conveniences in the studiolike bedroom.*

## CARPENTER'S DREAM HOUSE

Seventy-five years ago, Ichio Kumakura's grandfather built the house in the Imaguman quarter of Kyoto in which the carpenter now lives with his wife, Sachiko. A few years ago, Kumakura decided to use his woodworking skills to renovate the building without changing its original characteristics, allowing the place to retain its rustic charm.

*Left: Thick stone steps leading up to the front entrance of the house, overscale pots, a small bamboo bench to sit on while removing one's shoes, a pond filled with carp, and a sliver of a garden are evocative exterior elements of the modest house.*

*Right: In the entrance foyer, the floor is covered with sisal matting woven in a decorative pattern. The window at the rear has bars made of bamboo.*

**Left and Above:** *The main tatami-covered living space opens onto the garden.*

**Right:** *A small cabinet holds china used for the tea ceremony.*

**Below and Below Right:** *The hallways are lined with a series of sliding panels.*

## TIMELESS INN

The Tawaraya in Kyoto, one of Japan's most distinguished *ryokans,* or inns, has been in the same family for 11 generations. With its well-appointed tatami rooms, old-fashioned bathrooms, and lovely, manicured garden, the inn seems not to have changed in centuries and still offers a glimpse of the time-honored Japanese way of life.

*Left:* The Tawaraya Inn is located on a Kyoto street. In the past, horses were tied to the bamboo hitching posts.

*Below Far Left:* A lantern stands by the entrance.

*Below Center Left:* The courtyard has a granite floor that is always kept wet and shiny.

*Below Left:* Wide-plank wood floors line the hallways.

*Bottom Far Left, Bottom Center Left, and Bottom Left:* A wooden post set in stone, a granite head, and a vase of flowers are some of the refinements of the inn.

*Right:* At the end of the hall, a stone basin is the decorative focus of a tiny courtyard.

***Above:*** *During the day, a dining table and low chairs are set up in one of the tatami rooms. At night, they are put aside and replaced with a futon for sleeping.*

**Above:** *Although equipped with new ceramic tile and hardware, the bathroom still retains a traditional wooden tub.*

# LOOKING WEST

Nothing seems more evident in modern Japan than the influence of the Western way of life. Western styles in clothing, food, and especially in home design appear tantalizingly exotic to the Japanese, and also represent a freer attitude. Sitting on chairs around the dining room table, lounging on a leather sofa, cooking in an American-style efficiency kitchen, and collecting European antiques are only some of the common practices that reflect Japan's assimilation of Western culture.

Often there is a complex combination of two worlds. The guest room of a starkly modern house is furnished in the traditional manner, with a futon to be used by visiting relatives set down on the tatami-covered floor. And often, even the most modern house still retains a tea-ceremony room. While many foreign residents of Japan embrace the traditional Oriental ways, it is the well-traveled and sophisticated Japanese who frequently opt to live in a Westernized style.

But adopting a Western point of view involves more than simply choosing a different style of furnishings. It also means making decisions about how to live in a certain interior. In the fashion designer Junko Koshino's minimalist Tokyo duplex, the spacious lower floor was designed for Western-style entertaining while the self-contained upper floor retains the intimacy and privacy typical of Japanese family life.

*Far Left and Left: Western style is reflected in a postmodern house by the architect Shin Takamatsu, as well as in a selection of contemporary seating.*

## DOUBLE DUTY DUPLEX

The design planned by Tokyo-based architect Shigeru Uchida was based on separating the rooms used for family life from those meant to function as spaces for public entertaining. Situated in a small building on one of Tokyo's most fashionable shopping streets, the apartment belongs to Junko Koshino, a fashion designer, and her family.

The duplex is enormous by Tokyo standards. A Japanese pink, gray, and black granite is used throughout the sleek, minimally furnished open space. On the lower level, a large living room, dining area, and small kitchen are meant for parties and receptions. The bedrooms, a master bath, as well as a spacious eat-in family kitchen are on the more private second floor.

*Above:* The duplex is located in a newly built apartment house.

*Far Left:* On the lower floor, a small efficiency kitchen is adjacent to a dining area and spacious living room.

*Below Far Left:* Simple black leather upholstered furniture provides seating in the living area, which is used primarily for entertaining. The floor is of highly polished pink, gray, and black granite.

*Left:* Small black towels are arranged beside the place settings on the low coffee table.

*Right and Below Right:* One of
the walls of the lower floor is lined
entirely with hardwareless
cabinets in which are stored
Junko Koshino's extensive
collection of antique porcelain,
ceramic pieces, and lacquerware.

**Left:** *Two kettles stand on a stainless-steel kitchen counter that is edged in granite.*

**Below Left:** *A long sliver of a window allows daylight into a corner of the lower floor.*

*Above:* A large stainless-steel hood hangs over the cooking grill that has been set into the table in the upstairs family kitchen.

*Above:* A pair of chopsticks and five fish form a composition on a ceramic plate.

*Right:* Colanders and cooking utensils are set out on a counter in the kitchen.

**Above:** On the upper floor, the Western-style bathroom features overscale matte-gray tiles.

**Right:** A sandblasted glass panel diffuses the light over the bathroom sink.

*Left and Below Left:* The wide stair that links the two floors of the duplex is lined by a glass-paneled railing.

## APARTMENT FOR ART NOUVEAU

For the last 25 years, Noboru Kurisaki, who is known as one of the best flower arrangers in Japan, has been an ardent collector of Art Nouveau objects. Every French or English antique table in Kurisaki's tastefully furnished Tokyo apartment seems to be topped with a Tiffany lamp, a rare piece of Gallé art glass, or a precious bronze period figurine. By contrast, Kurisaki's tea-ceremony room is purely Japanese — and a perfect example of the traditional genre.

*Above: A plant-filled container is just outside the front door of the apartment.*

*Left and Right: The mixture of objects in Noboru Kurisaki's duplex apartment includes both Japanese and European artworks and antiques. A drawing by Tsuguhara Fujita and a screen by Kuniyoshi Kaneko are displayed with such collector's items as a 19th-century carved mahogany sofa, an antique gaming table, and an extraordinary sculpted Art Nouveau hall unit.*

***Above and Right:*** *Noboru Kurisaki has a special tea-ceremony room in his apartment where visitors come to learn the ancient and disciplined tradition. The step-by-step rules of the* Cha-no-yu, *or tea ceremony, are called* temae *and include setting out the utensils, cleaning them, warming the tea bowls and small bamboo whisk, and preparing and serving the tea.*

*Above:* The bedroom is situated on the lower level of the apartment. An antique kimono lies on the bed. The telephone, clock, and television are set on the floor.

*Left:* Bronze sculptures of crabs and a bouquet of grasses create a whimsical underwater tableau in the bathtub.

## CALIFORNIA STYLE

The pied-à-terre and guest house that the designer Shiro Kuramata renovated for Esprit, the international clothing company, is located in the center of Tokyo but has a surprisingly bucolic feeling.

The California-style house sits on a hilly site surrounded by tall trees. A wide terrace integrates the landscape with the interior. Kuramata unified the spaces by using his signature material – a nougatlike terrazzo with chips of glass that reflect and catch the light.

**Above:** *A wide terrace stretches along the length of the house.*

**Left:** *Floor-to-ceiling glass doors are the only barriers between the exterior and the interior.*

*Right:* Tea is served alfresco on simple metal outdoor furniture.

*Far Right:* A cube-shaped studio and gatehouse is at the entrance to the property. The green panel is a shuttered window that can be opened to accept deliveries.

*Right:* Shiro Kuramata's terrazzo material is used on the ground floor throughout the modern house.

*Far Right:* The stainless-steel and glass umbrella stand beside the front door is also by the designer.

**Above:** *Terrazzo has also been used for the large square coffee table in the living room. Canvas shades control the light.*

**Right:** *The chrome-framed three-seater sofa by Shiro Kuramata is paired with an Italian floor lamp by Achille Castiglioni.*

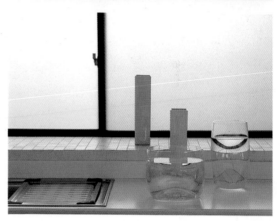

**Top and Above:** *The kitchen has been outfitted with both Japanese and Western accessories.*

**Left:** *Cane chairs surround the table in the Western-style kitchen.*

**Far Left:** *An angled stair leads to the second floor, where the bedrooms are situated.*

**Left, Below Far Left, Below Left, and Right:** *One of the guest rooms has been furnished in the traditional Japanese style. Tatami mats cover the floor and pillows provide seating.*

## WESTERNIZED RESIDENCE

The centuries-old gatehouses and rice warehouses were the only buildings preserved on an estate in the town of Kawaguchi when Shigeyuki and Sumiko Nakayama asked the architect Mayumi Miyawaki to design a modern house on the site of the family mansion. Having grown up on the property, Nakayama decided that he now wanted to live in a Westernized residence that would be contemporary but not too avant-garde.

Although the exterior has many elements that refer to traditional Japanese architecture, the interior, furnished with classic modern European pieces by Le Corbusier, Joe Colombo, and Eileen Gray, is Occidental.

*Above Left:* The exterior of the house, with its peaked roofs, is intentionally traditional.

*Left:* The main access to the building is through the old gateway.

*Below Left:* A plump modern armchair can be glimpsed in one of the bedrooms.

*Right and Center Right:* The gridlike front door is framed in glass.

*Above Far Right:* The steel fireplace is one of the house's typically Western elements.

*Right:* The rice warehouse in the garden has been restored.

*Center Right:* The all-gray combination office and media room is furnished in a contemporary style.

*Far Right:* A sliding red pocket door closes off the living room from the hall.

**Above:** *The sofa and chair by Le Corbusier, as well as the floor lamp by Joe Colombo, contribute to the Western look of the living room.*

**Right:** *The different parts of the house are arranged around a small interior court.*

*Left and Below Left:* Only the guest room – frequently used by visiting relatives – is traditional. Tatami mats cover the floor and futons and quilts are stored in the cupboards during the day, to be brought out at night.

## GALLERY-HOME FOR SCULPTURE

Because the Tokyo house was to function as a gallery and home for Shin Aoki, a designer and manufacturer of stainless-steel and brass sculpture, Arata Isozaki, one of Japan's most prominent architects, felt it was appropriate to include metal in the construction. Completed about seven years ago, the building is one of the most striking examples of Isozaki's residential projects.

The four-story house with concrete walls is distinguished by its imposing barrel-vaulted living room. Black is the predominating color for the furnishings – emphasizing the sensual semidarkness of the main living space.

*Above: The exterior view of the concrete house is that of a simple cube. Shin Aoki's sculpture gallery is on the street level.*

*Left: The main living space on the top floor is dominated by an arched ceiling and huge circular window.*

*Right:* The overscale black leather-covered sofa by the Italian architect Vico Magistretti seems dwarfed by the imposing spatial architecture.

*Below:* The small house has been custom-designed to fit into a narrow site on a heavily trafficked street.

*Bottom:* A matching set of time and temperature pieces is hung on the wall.

**Above:** Circular stereo speakers are inset into the wall of polished granite that separates the kitchen from the living area.

**Right:** The sinuous high-backed side chair was designed by architect Arata Isozaki.

154

**Above:** *The modern eat-in kitchen is of Western inspiration. Dishes are stored in a large cubelike cabinet and the appliances are lined up under the bay window.*

## GLAMOROUS HIGH RISE

Françoise Morechand first came to Japan from Paris in 1958. After spending a decade in New York and returning to Tokyo 12 years ago, she has established herself as one of that city's most renowned television and radio personalities. She is also an author in Japanese of a dozen best-selling women's lifestyle books, and a textile designer who specializes in kimonos.

Morechand and her husband, Tatsuji Nagataki, a rock music producer, live in the center of Tokyo in a glamorous high-rise penthouse apartment. In the large space, Morechand has audaciously mixed the old-fashioned family heirlooms that she brought with her from Europe with contemporary Japanese art objects – many of which are the work of the couple's artist friends.

*Above Left:* The sofa is placed against the floor-to-ceiling windows, which offer a dramatic view of Tokyo's busy freeways.

*Far Left:* The glass coffee table holds some of Françoise Morechand's collection of cat figures and china tea bowls.

*Above Left and Left:* A tablecloth of traditional indigo cotton covers the dining table, which is set with unmatched pieces of rare antique china and Baccarat crystal goblets.

*Right:* The all-white living room includes an eclectic mixture of country French furniture, modern upholstered sofas, neoclassical plaster busts, and palm trees.

*Left:* Ceremonial kimonos
designed by Françoise Morechand
are folded on a low table in front of
an antique European chest.

*Right:* A contemporary ceramic by Shozo Furukawa has been placed under the watchful eye of Morechand's great-grandmother.

## ARCHITECTURAL PRESERVATION

Bernard and Tamiko Cendron (he is an executive with Cartier, Inc., in Japan) live with their children in a residential quarter of Tokyo. Their historic house, which was built about 50 years ago by Antonin Raymond, is one of the few remaining buildings by the architect who worked with Frank Lloyd Wright and stayed on in Japan after such projects as the Imperial Hotel were completed.

Although the Cendrons added their own French period furnishings to the interior, they kept the custom-built wood cabinets and paneling intact and had the Art Deco-style rice-paper panels reproduced to restore the house to its original design.

Also original is the dramatic entrance to the house, through a covered courtyard where a path of rugged rocks leads past a flourishing persimmon tree.

*Above:* A wooden gate separates the house and courtyard from the street.

*Left:* The front door is half hidden at the end of the courtyard.

**Above:** *Stone steps and a pathway of rocks lead up to the entrance.*

**Right:** *A large sculptural rock sits on a pedestal near the house.*

**Far Right:** *Low stools provide seating in the back garden.*

**Below Right:** *A screen of bamboo grows at the rear of the house.*

**Below Far Right:** *The wood-paneled entrance hall features original built-in storage units.*

*Top:* Shoji screens open onto the Western-style dining room.

*Above:* The living room is focused on an iron wood-burning stove.

*Right:* A collection of antique blue-and-white porcelain is displayed in the living room. The rice-paper sliding doors were designed at the time the house was built.

**Above:** *The bathtub looks as if it has been carved out of a wall of rocks.*

**Above Left:** *A combination of Oriental floor pillows and European upholstery is used to furnish the living room, which offers a view of the back garden.*

**Left:** *A plush, silk-covered daybed is in a corner of the living room, under an antique Japanese panel.*

# DUAL FACADE

The most unusual feature of the modern house designed by architects Toshiroh and Akira Ikegami is its double facade. Facing the street is a slightly forbidding wall of cement with an angular bay window; the other facade, opening onto a gravel-covered garden, has more rounded architectural forms.

The interior of the Osaka house is sparse, with a modern American-style kitchen and seating reduced to a simple pillowed sofa.

*Left:* The back facade of the cement house has a rounded bay window and floor-to-ceiling windows that face a stone courtyard.

*Right:* A peaked roof, glass block, metal railings, and windows set at an angle above the front door are decorative architectural details that emphasize the postmodern look of the house.

*Right:* Modern chairs and a wood table, as well as a low upholstered sofa, are nearly the only pieces of furniture in the combination living and dining room.

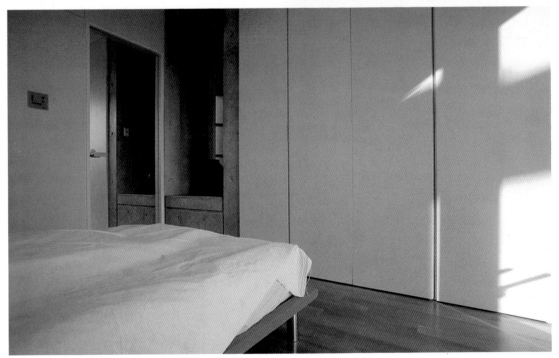

*Above:* One of the bedrooms has been set up in the Western style, with a mattress permanently raised on a platform.

*Right:* The open kitchen has rounded custom-designed storage units. The sink and cook top are recessed into stainless-steel-topped counters.

**Above:** *The Japanese, tatami-floor bedroom is serene. Hardwareless doors cover the closets and opaque window blinds diffuse the light.*

**Left:** *One side of the door has been mirrored to give the illusion of extra space.*

# SECLUDED RESIDENCE

Born in 1905 in Kyoto, Seiichi Sirai was one of the *éminences grises* of modern Japanese architecture and, especially since his death in 1983, has been considered a cult figure for the current generation of architects.

Among the first to integrate Western culture and artifacts into the traditional Japanese house, Sirai lived and worked in a secluded private residence hidden behind a high, forbidding gate. The interior of the building in the north of Tokyo is intentionally dark and insulated from the outside world.

Eighteenth-century French furniture, an ancient Greek sculpture head, and a Romanesque capital in the extraordinary Zen garden are three examples of the master's unusual sensibilities.

*Right: All the elements that are included in the approach to the house emphasize its sense of seclusion. A wall lines the street; the slot for the newspaper is inserted into a brick surface; and the doorbell is set into a rough stone wall.*

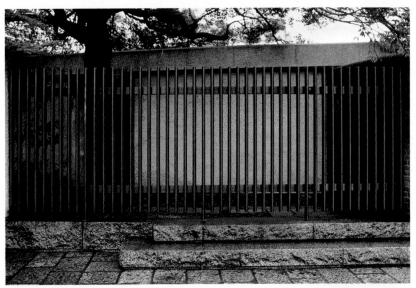

*Left:* A 19th-century Belgian chest and an ancient Greek head are some of the European pieces in the house.

*Below Left:* Set on a late-18th-century French chest, a candle casts an atmospheric glow in the dimly lit interior.

*Below:* Two silk-shaded lamps stand on the desk in architect Seiichi Sirai's private office.

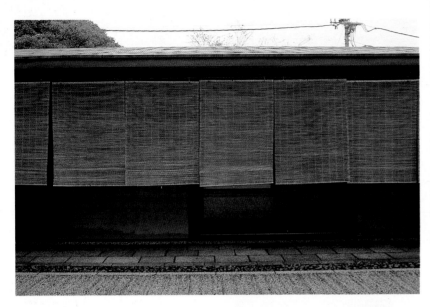

**Above:** Roll-up bamboo slatted blinds create a sense of separation between the house and the adjoining garden.

**Below:** Different-sized rocks and stones provide a play of patterns in the space between the house and the meditation garden.

**Above and Right:** A Romanesque capital brought back from London has been chosen as the central focus of the Zen garden.

## PERFECTLY MINIMAL

Formerly part of the Cuban Embassy compound in Tokyo, the house renovated by Maxine Van-Cliffe, an English fashion stylist and public relations executive, and her husband, Hiroyuki Arakawa, a fashion photographer, is a spare, lustrous space in which every detail – from the nails to the tiles – was chosen by the occupants with obsessive care.

Van-Cliffe, who has lived in Japan for nearly 20 years and is fluent in Japanese, worked as the general contractor on the project, searching out light fixtures from Italy, stereo equipment from Scandinavia, and kitchen appliances from Germany. Because the interior was to be minimal, particular attention was paid to such elements as the shiny polyurethaned floors, polished granite countertops, and laboratorylike white tiles.

*Above and Left: Behind a metal gate, an exterior stair leads up to the entrance.*

*Above Right and Far Right: A greenhouselike enclosure extends the living space of the house.*

*Right: The slatted front door opens into a small triangular entrance foyer.*

Hamano Institute

ART WORKSHOP

K Architect & Associates

ARAKAWA
HIROYUKI & MAXINE

**Above:** *An angled step marks the change in floor material from polished wood parquet to white ceramic tile.*

**Above Right:** *The front door is framed by two matching windows. White ceramic tile extends into the front hall.*

**Right and Far Right:** *One of the windows opens into the sleek kitchen, which is equipped with granite countertops and all-white cabinetry.*

**Above:** *The sofa at one end of the living room has been covered in a crinkled silklike fabric. The small pink metal Italian table by Achille Castiglioni is among the only touches of color.*

**Left:** *Except for the stereo equipment against one wall and a few books stacked up on the highly polished floor, the main area of the living room is completely empty. The large painting is by Duggie Fields, an English artist.*

*Above:* A narrow curving stair leads to the second floor.

*Above Right and Right:* The simple railing on the landing has been painted gray, as have the doors and built-in cabinetry in the bedroom.

**Above:** A multidrawer chest, paired with an African sculpture, stands at the end of the second-floor landing.

**Above Left:** The master bedroom is minimally furnished. A hardwareless cabinet doubles as a headboard. The fixtures in the corners provide atmospheric lighting.

**Left:** With its Western bathtub and double sinks, the bathroom is luxuriously appointed. White ceramic tiles cover the floor and walls.

*Above: Kimiaki Ashino's collection of black shoes is neatly lined up on the black ceramic-tiled floor just inside the front door.*

*Left: The design of the concrete house was influenced by the modernist architecture of the 1920s and '30s.*

## ALL BLACK AND WHITE

Kimiaki Ashino, an art book publisher and book dealer, was not an architect but knew exactly what he wanted when he had a house built in the Okusawa residential suburb of Tokyo.

Influenced by the architect R. M. Schindler, who is best known for his modernist work in California, Ashino designed a geometric concrete structure with a rigorously black-and-white interior. Classic modern pieces of furniture and high-tech industrial materials are used creatively to achieve the striking early 20th-century machine-age look.

*Above: Black ceramic tiles, set on the diagonal, cover the steps that lead from the front gate up to the entrance of the house.*

*Above:* The grand piano in the living room belongs to Kimiaki Ashino's wife, Tomoko, a musicologist. An old-fashioned gramophone that dates from 1928 looms behind the sofa by Eileen Gray. An extensive collection of 78 rpm records is kept in especially designed drawers.

*Above:* Two Bibendum armchairs by Eileen Gray, one upholstered in black leather, the other in white, carry out the monochromatic scheme of the house.

*Left:* Black and white ceramic tiles of different sizes and laid in a variety of patterns are the focus of the Western-style bathroom.

183

*Above:* A chair by Le Corbusier has been pulled up to the sink in the mezzanine bedroom.

*Above:* Metal shelves hold Kimiaki Ashino's collection of art books in the corner of the master bedroom that has been turned into a library and work area.

*Right:* A Bauhaus fabric covers the bed, which has been placed on a platform overlooking the library.

*Top and Above:* The small building is set on a corner in the center of Tokyo. The main entrance to the duplex is in the back, up a short flight of stairs.

*Above Right:* The bowls of salt and water in front of the window are part of a Shinto religious ritual.

*Right:* A circular metal stair links the living room to the bedrooms above. The floor is covered in easy-to-maintain white ceramic tile.

## INTERNATIONAL STYLE

African sculpture, Italian chairs, 300-year-old Japanese pottery, and prints by David Hockney and Jim Dine are some of the elements in the family house that belongs to Seiichi Mizuno, the general manager of the Seibu department stores' Shibuya branch, and his wife, Maki, a restaurateur who specializes in Japanese nouvelle cuisine.

The exterior of the building in the Yotsuya section of Tokyo was designed by Yoshio Sasaki about seven years ago. The international-style interior, designed by the Mizunos themselves, is the result of the couple's travels and their sophisticated lifestyle.

*Far Left: The mixture of furnishings in the living room includes low Japanese lacquered tables, African sculpture, and Italian chrome and leather chairs.*

*Left: The chair in the bedroom is a 1960s Japanese design.*

*Below Left: A low cabinet doubles as a head-board for the freestanding Western-style bed.*

**Left:** *The family's valuable small antiques and objects used for the tea ceremony are kept in a 150-year-old hardwood chest.*

**Right:** *When the doors of the chest are open, they reveal stacked boxes that are often as important as the objects they protect.*

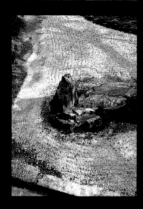

## SMALL SPACES

Making the most of a small space is a talent of Japanese city dwellers. The density of the population and the high prices of real estate have forced them to live in what Westerners would consider impossibly diminutive spaces.

"A Japanese can make a whole life in a small space," noted Tadeo Ando, a modern architect, referring to the way even a tiny room can be arranged so as to provide all the necessary comforts. Discipline and neatness are prime requirements, as is a willingness to live with only the essentials in multipurpose rooms, where futons are brought out of closets or chests to sleep on at night.

An innovation for dealing with tiny spaces, apart from clever storage solutions, has been to build vertically, stacking rooms one atop the other, with a single space to each floor – as in the architect Takamitsu Azuma's pioneering minitower, or Kazuhiro Ishii's graceful small town house built on the site of a ginkgo tree. It is an approach that culminates in Osaka architect's Yasuo Yoshida's inventive multicolor maze of intersecting catwalks.

*Far Left and Left: In most Japanese gardens, the lack of space has inspired the creation of miniature as well as symbolic landscapes, in which stones are as important as plants.*

## TREE HOUSE

When Kazuhiro Ishii, a young architect, went to see a piece of land for sale in the Akasaka section of Tokyo, he found that a five-story-high ginkgo tree was growing in the middle of the tiny lot, once the site of a temple. After obtaining permission to cut down the tree, Ishii designed a minuscule residence for himself, one room to a floor, all contained within the 330-square-foot plot.

Inside, furnishings are kept to a minimum. The walls of the bedroom on the basement floor are insulated with goose-down quilting to protect the interior from the cold in winter and the humidity in the summer; a narrow staircase links all the spaces, including the second-floor living room, workroom, and kitchen, and the tea-ceremony room on the third floor.

In the entrance foyer, an inset granite floor recalls the site of the tree, and the remaining stump is enshrined in a corner.

*Left: A model of Kazuhiro Ishii's tiny house is displayed on the stump of the ginkgo tree in the hall. The glass of water is an element of a religious homage to the tree, which was originally part of a shrine.*

*Top Right, Above Right, and Right: Concrete and glass block are the two main materials used in the house.*

*Far Right: Shoes are lined up near the front door. The granite inset in the floor marks the original site of the ginkgo tree.*

*Above:* The plants on the terrace cast soft shadows through the translucent screens.

*Above Left:* The glass door at the end of the hall creates an illusion of extra space.

*Left:* The narrow open stair has steps covered in sisal matting and a thin metal railing.

*Right:* Goose down is used for the vertical window blinds as well as for wall coverings in the second-floor combination living room, workroom, and kitchen.

*Left:* The bed takes up nearly the whole room in the basement bedroom. Goose down is used throughout – as insulation on the walls as well as for the comforter and pillows on the bed.

*Below Left and Right:* The tea-ceremony room is at the top of the house. The peaked roof is lined with goose down, and the windows covered with rice-paper panels. A stove has been set in the tatami-mat-covered floor, and the accessories for the preparation of tea are stored behind sliding doors.

197

## FOREIGN IDYLL

Pierre Baudry, a French marketing consultant whose first trip to Japan dates from 20 years ago, calls his diminutive and traditionally Japanese Tokyo residence "my country house." For although small in scale, the house has a proportionately large garden and offers a peaceful and well-ordered way of life that many Europeans living in Japan find easy to embrace.

*Right:* The corner house is half hidden behind a low wall of cement bricks.

*Below Right and Below Far Right:* Inside the front door, the foyer leads directly to a narrow corridor.

*Below Right:* The garden extends the living space of the small house.

*Far Right:* Storage is provided by an antique Oriental cabinet, which because of its size had to be placed in the gallery.

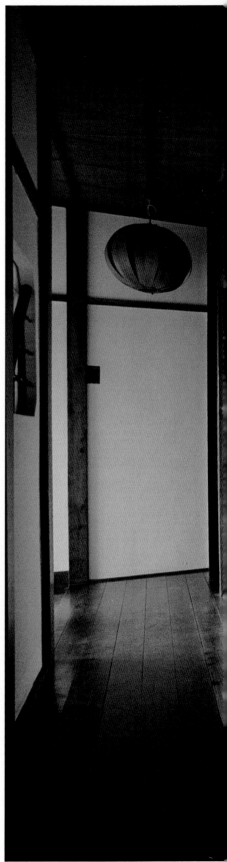

**Above:** The large dining table is raised over a pit in the floor that provides leg room for diners.

**Left:** Floor pillows covered in batik are stacked in a corner of the living room when not in use.

*Above:* A small desk in the gallery takes advantage of the view.

*Right:* Because the foundation of the house is raised, it is necessary to step down into the garden.

**Above:** *The shallow bathroom sink is lined with ceramic tile. The reassembled broken mirror is Pierre Baudry's handiwork.*

**Left and Right:** *A thick comforter covers the futon on the floor in the bedroom. The modern engraving on wood of a geisha is by Tsuguhara Fujita. The vegetables are part of a religious offering.*

## INTERSECTING PLANES

The interior of the Osaka house in which furniture designer Taizo Kim lives with his wife, Masako Shiomi, an illustrator, and their small son, Ipoh, is an inspiring study in space-stretching devices.

Yasuo Yoshida, a young Osaka-based architect, designed and built the house, using prefabricated industrial elements. The complex system of see-through metal mezzanines and catwalks that connect the different levels not only allows air and light to circulate throughout the space but also provides for an exciting visual and spatial experience.

*Above:* The narrow ceramic tile-fronted house is on a small side street in Osaka.

*Right:* Industrial metal grating is used for the stairs, floors, and railings.

**Far Left:** *Taizo Kim crafted the slat-back chairs that surround the dining table.*

**Left:** *An ornate antique chest contrasts with the ruggedness of the concrete wall.*

**Below Far Left:** *Outside the bathroom, a ladderlike stair leads to the master bedroom.*

**Below Left:** *The very narrow bathroom has an open shower and an illusionistic black and white checked floor.*

*Above:* The view up toward the roof of the house is dizzying. Metal grid floors and railings emphasize the feeling of openness.

**Above:** *Seen from above, a web of catwalks links the different areas of the interior.*

## TWO TINY ROOMS

Kaoru Watanabe, an advertising art director, has only two tiny rooms in a modern apartment building in the chic Daikanyama residential area of Tokyo. Nevertheless, he is an avid collector of Japanese, Chinese, and Korean antiques as well as classic modern upholstered pieces.

*Above:* The living room is furnished with modern pieces by Le Corbusier, Eileen Gray, and Vico Magistretti.

*Left:* An English metal lamp from the 1950s, a Japanese bronze of a horse and jockey, and an antique Chinese horse are among the objects displayed on the glass-topped desk.

*Above:* Boxes of porcelains are stacked up on an antique cabinet.

*Right:* A poem by Kaou, a Japanese poet, lies across a piece of 19th-century pottery.

**Above:** *The Chinese cabinet is part of Kaoru Watanabe's collection of Oriental antiques.*

**Left:** *A large antique Japanese bowl sits on the floor under the desk.*

## SUBURBAN ROW HOUSE

Yoichi and Sumiko Nishimura are a recently married couple who live in one of a series of modern row houses in Daita, a suburb of Tokyo. The diminutive residence includes a kitchen and eating area on the entrance level, and a mezzanine living room. A narrow metal stair leads to the bedroom on the lower level.

A collection of objects – vintage toys and antique kitchen tools – as well as stripped pine furniture and elaborate stereo equipment are indications of the young couple's fashionable interests.

*Top Left, Top Center, Above Left, and Above:* A cement arch acts as a ceremonial entrance to Casa Volar, a small-scaled development of town houses for eight young families. The mailboxes are staggered on a wall parallel to the stairs shared by all the buildings.

*Top Right:* A monumental television set takes up the most space in the living room.

*Above Right and Right:* The table-top in the dining area is made from terrazzo by Shiro Kuramata. Stereo components are stacked up to face the living area.

*Left:* Antique kitchen tools, including two scales and a grinder, and hanging garlic bulbs, peppers, and dried ears of corn decorate the dollhouse-size stove.

*Far Left:* A metal dockplate stair connects the living space on the upper floor to the bedroom below.

*Left:* The quilt-covered futon sits directly on the bedroom floor.

*Below Left:* Antique toys are arranged on an English stripped pine chest.

*Right:* An Ikebana flower arrangement is displayed on an antique Japanese chest in the living room.

## PERSONAL REFUGE

Located in one of Tokyo's newer buildings, the two-room apartment was transformed by Michiko Kitamura, an avant-garde fashion stylist, from a tiny and ordinary space into an intimate, personal refuge that pays tribute to the meditative values of the traditional Japanese interior.

Blue and white antique fabrics are used throughout, creating a secluded, tentlike environment that isolates its occupant from the outside world.

*Above:* A piece of antique fabric is draped over an Oriental chest in Michiko Kitamura's tiny Tokyo apartment.

*Left:* Blue and white fabrics function as ad hoc room dividers and increase the illusion of space.

*Above:* A photograph and some pieces of ancient Japanese pottery are displayed on a decorative chest.

*Right:* The harsh daylight is diffused by the traditional shoji screens in front of which are hung half curtains called noren.

217

*Left:* In the winter, the dining table is covered with a quilt to provide warmth for people seated on the floor around it.

*Right:* At night, a futon is unfolded on the floor for sleeping in the living room that doubles as a bedroom.

*Above:* Antique Korean and Chinese chests and cabinets are lined up next to one another.

*Above Right and Right:* A pomegranate in a porcelain bowl and a stone set on a lacquer tray are two of the stylistic still lifes in the small apartment.

*Far Right:* A corner of the room has been turned into a comfortable reading area.

219

## VERTICAL SPACE

It was nearly 20 years ago that Takamitsu Azuma built Tower House, a tiny residence in which the Osaka-born architect lives with his wife, Setsuko. The rough concrete structure is located on a 200-square-foot lot in the center of Tokyo.

A concrete gateway, narrow parking space, and stone steps lead up to the front door, behind which are nestled the kitchen and a seating area. A narrow spiral stair connects the ground-floor level to the upstairs bedrooms and a bathroom. All the objects of domestic daily life – from books to pots and pans – are crammed into the tiny vertical space. The house is a startling example of the inventive discipline required to live in such tight quarters.

*Left and Above Right: Tower House is a small concrete building in the center of Tokyo.*

*Right: The book-lined study is at the top of the narrow house.*

*Below Right: A spiral stair links the floors.*

*Far Right: The seating area is close to the cluttered kitchen.*

*Far Right: The master bedroom is situated on the second-floor landing. A portable electric heater provides warmth in the winter months.*

## THE CRAFT TRADITION

Most first-time visitors to Japan no doubt tend to look more toward the past than the future. In a country where the distinction between craft and art does not really apply, centuries-old techniques of making pottery, lacquerware, screens, kimonos, and calligraphy – Japanese crafts that are famous throughout the world – still survive as reminders of the continuity with the past. Many other traditions are today being rediscovered – whether it be constructing houses with wood joints rather than nails to express a reverence toward trees, or creating such complex textiles as hand-woven silks laced with gold and silver threads, and elegantly patterned indigo-dyed cottons.

One of the finest and most influential Japanese crafts on an international scale is that of pottery, where the functional is perfectly integrated with the decorative. The importance of the tea ceremony and the many different pieces of china needed for Japanese food have been practical reasons for sustaining the art. And while in the West calligraphy is considered a minor art, in Japan it remains as a singularly refined and artistic mode of expression.

*Far Left and Left: At the Open Air Museum of Old Japanese Farmhouses, near Osaka, the ancient craft of house building is represented in the peaked roofs of the reconstructed buildings.*

## MASTER POTTER'S LEGACY

Until his death in his eighties, Shoji Hamada was known as one of Japan's living national treasures. For over 50 years he was considered among the most famous and inventive craftsmen of his time, a potter and artist who reinterpreted the traditional craft by infusing it with his own creativity and new techniques.

Hamada lived and worked in Mashiko, a town north of Tokyo, on a large compound that included a gatehouse, workshop, and residence. His home was the result of his commitment to traditional Japanese values and his exposure as a young man to European culture. A collector as well as a craftsman, Hamada was influenced by such artists as the English potter Bernard Leach and filled his home with favorite pieces in addition to his own work. Today, the familiar clay material is still being piled behind the workshop in 10-foot-high mounds, as Hamada's family carries on in the steps of the master.

*Above and Right: Potter Shoji Hamada's house was originally a traditional Japanese* minka, *or farmhouse.*

*Left: Topiary bushes line the path near the property's gatehouse.*

**Left:** *The front door opens onto a sparsely furnished interior, with shiny wood floors and large windows that allow views through the entire house.*

**Right:** *One of Shoji Hamada's large clay pots that has been glazed stands in the hallway.*

*Left:* Some of the master potter's pieces are mingled with his personal collection of favorite works that are displayed throughout the main house.

*Right:* Large tansu chests function as dividers between the tatami-covered rooms of the craftsman's residence. Floor-to-ceiling rice-paper screens further add to the flexibility of the spaces.

228

## KIMONO WORKSHOP

Yoichi and Sue Sasaki live in one of the oldest quarters in Kyoto. Their craft is traditional Japanese costume design, and the couple work primarily for the theater and movies. One of their most recent projects was to make all the costumes for Akira Kurosawa's epic film *Ran*.

Every process – from the dyeing of the silk and the weaving of gold and silver threads to the embroidering of lavish designs and the creation of the finished garments – is done in their workroom according to the purest of craft traditions.

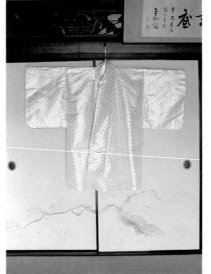

*Far Left: The workroom is at the end of a small courtyard.*

*Left: Ornate eaves are typical of town houses in Kyoto.*

*Below Far Left: Yoichi and Sue Sasaki sit on the tatami-covered floor of their office.*

*Below Left: The sliding screens are delicately detailed.*

*Bottom Far Left and Bottom Left: Two recently completed silk kimonos are on display.*

*Right: In the atelier, craftsmen work on the different steps needed to create the silk fabrics and opulent garments.*

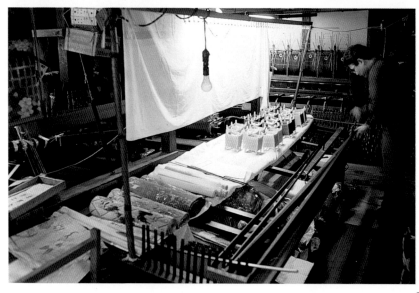

## OCEANSIDE CRAFTS COLLABORATION

The handcrafted house is situated on a hill in Hayama, near the oceanside resort of Kamakura, southeast of Tokyo. It was a two-year collaboration among its owner, Masao Tsuzi, a Japanese artist who creates Western-style oil paintings; the architect Takao Habuka; Toshio Yoshikawa, a wood craftsman and artisan; and Masahiro Tsuzi, the owner's son, a sculptor who works in metal.

From the ornate iron gate to the inlaid wood floor and hand-painted shoji screens, the house exemplifies how decoration and function work together.

*Left: The exterior of the house is of wood that has been stained black. All the fanciful wrought-iron and welded sculptural ironwork is by Masahiro Tsuzi. Bamboo plants also add a decorative element.*

*Below and Right: A huge vase of glazed pottery from the Momoyama period sits dramatically in midair on an openwork shelf in the stairwell.*

233

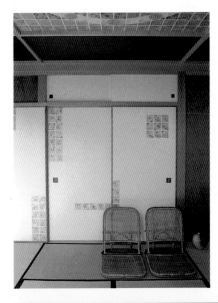

*Top Left and Top Right:* Masao Tsuzi painted the motifs on the rice-paper panels and ceiling mandala in the tatami room. The wrought-iron treelike sculpture by Kotaro Kurata seems to support the clerestory wall.

*Top Center:* The intricate wood parquet floor is a work of art by Toshio Yoshikawa.

*Above:* Beautifully crafted wood is the main material used in the interior. The living room can be glimpsed from the stair.

*Right:* Trunks from the kiaki tree, a hardwood, have been crafted into a low table in the living room.

## CALLIGRAPHER'S ART

One of Japan's oldest traditions, and one that is unfortunately disappearing, is that of the *rakugo* – the oral fairytale recited in a *yose,* a kind of theater, by a *rakugoka,* or storyteller.

Small posters announced these events to the public. Designing the posters has traditionally been the work of special calligraphers, and 83-year-old Ukon Tachibana is one of the last alive to practice the craft.

*Above: Calligrapher Ukon Tachibana stands in front of his house.*

*Right: Samples of calligraphy have been glued to the closet doors.*

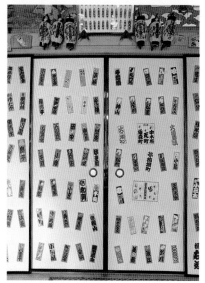

*Above Left and Far Left:* Two models of yose are displayed on shelves in the library.

*Above and Left:* The collage of engravings and illustrated stickers that decorates the artist's home is an example of his craft.

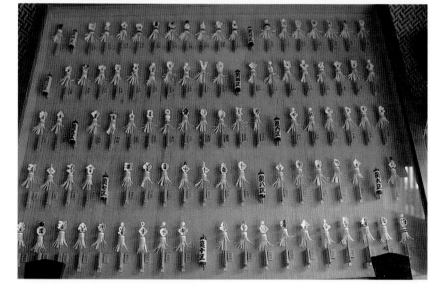

*Left:* A collection of miniature theater lamps has been neatly arranged and framed under glass.

*Top and Right:* Tachibana works seated on the floor.

*Above:* Colorful paper kites hang near the ceiling.

239

## MODERN TIMES

Trend-setting styles such as high-tech minimalism, American postmodernism, 1950s kitsch, and the Italian avant-garde look have found their enthusiasts in modern-day Japan. Like their Western counterparts, many young fashion-conscious Japanese are drawn to the exuberance and glamour of the Hollywood image, although still others prefer to adopt the stark minimalist esthetic. Lofts are being considered as alternative living places, and the taste for collectibles – whether Art Deco vases, Hawaiian shirts, rock 'n' roll memorabilia, antique toys, or conceptual art – has taken hold in Japan. Brightly colored and patterned graphics, innovative and experimental furniture, and imaginative reinterpretations of traditional elements also contribute to the verve and optimism of the style-conscious interiors.

*Far Left and Left:* Contemporary influences, from the machine age to 1950s kitsch and high-tech, are quickly integrated into everyday Japanese life.

## LOFT LIVING

The high-ceilinged loft in the Azabu-Juban area of Tokyo served as a warehouse for the fashion designer Yohji Yamamoto before Yoshihiko and Marcia Miko asked architect Naoki Iijima to convert it for residential use. The unusually large loft reflects the couple's taste for high-tech minimalism. He is a well-known fashion and advertising photographer, she is the art director for Jun, a Japanese fashion company, and they both travel often between Tokyo and New York.

*Left:* Antique wooden cooking and serving pieces are set on the floor near the loft's open kitchen.

*Right:* A black dining room chair creates a striking silhouette against one of the windows.

*Far Left:* The entrance hall is a stark introduction to the loft.

*Center Left:* Nylon string cafe chairs surround a dining table made from rough-hewn planks.

*Left:* The red-lacquered antique chest dates from the Edo period.

*Below Far Left:* Fluorescent light fixtures illuminate the photography studio area.

*Below Center Left:* A leather armchair by Le Corbusier provides seating in the living area.

*Below Left:* A vintage file cabinet has been wall-hung in the studio.

*Right:* The main living space – with its cement columns, painted floors, and visible electrical conduits – is typical of the high-tech loft esthetic.

*Below Right:* Canvas draperies separate the studio from the private living area. The frosted window was once the truck door of the loft.

## TOY WORLD

In the last 12 years, Teruhisa Kitahara has become the largest collector of robots in Japan. The author of a number of books on the subject, Kitahara has also founded a private museum of robots and antique toys called Toys Club, which is installed on the ground floor of his house in Yokohama.

*Above:* Teruhisa Kitahara stands in front of the window of his toy museum.

*Above Center Right:* A collection of animated clocks lines the stairs.

*Above Far Right:* On the landing, visitors are welcomed by a rabbit automaton.

*Right and Far Right:* The mixture of objects on the desk and in the vitrine includes a globe, a metal airplane, and Japanese comic strip characters from the 1930s.

*Left and Below Left:* An old gramophone, an ornate chandelier, a Louis Vuitton trunk, and antique clocks are some of Kitahara's eclectic objects.

*Top and Above: The antique robot with a mask and the robot with a baby are both Japanese.*

*Above Left: The stair railing holds a series of Peco Chan dolls – toys that were famous in the 1950s.*

*Left: Antique cars, airplanes, zeppelins, boats, and locomotives are some of the vintage toys on view in the museum.*

*Top, Above, and Right: A helmeted robot and a Bibendum-man-shaped robot are part of Kitahara's extraordinary collection of mechanical men that are neatly arranged on shelves.*

## GRAPHIC DESIGN

When Isao Tsunoi, a Tokyo-based graphic designer, had the opportunity to build a new house for himself and his wife, Mihoko, he planned an interior that would reflect his interest in the Italian avant-garde design movement known as Memphis. And even though the property was quite small, the couple still wanted their house to feel spacious.

Architect Isamu Kujirai designed the small square building in which a generously proportioned and high-ceilinged main living space was created at the expense of the kitchen and bedroom areas. The result is an airy white expanse that serves as a background for the Tsunois' esoteric and colorful assemblage of furniture and objects.

*Left:* The small square house is situated on a quiet side street.

*Left and Below Left:* A stair leads to the open mezzanine and the two bedrooms.

*Right:* Tall glass windows line two sides of the main living space. Chairs by Arne Jacobsen are paired with a glass-topped table. The floor is covered in white ceramic tile.

**Above:** *A trolley is stored under the mezzanine near the kitchen.*

**Left:** *The tiny courtyard, with its black-and-white tiled floor, is a graphic reinterpretation of a Japanese garden.*

*Above:* Ceramic pieces from the 1950s are assembled at the top of a storage unit.

*Right:* In the main living space there is a huge clock designed by Isao Tsunoi, as well as leopard-patterned pillows and a column covered in a Memphis-inspired trompe l'oeil pattern.

*Right:* A corner functions as a work area in one of the bedrooms and overlooks the floor below.

## FASHION STATEMENT

Rei Kawakubo, the creator of Comme des Garçons, the avant-garde Japanese fashion company, has designed a working environment that reflects her influential design philosophy – a synthesis of Oriental sparseness and hard-edge functionalism. The result is a rigorously monochromatic and minimalist interior.

*Left and Right: In the main reception room, the walls are of polished cement, the floor black and shiny, and furniture upholstered in black leather. A huge lamp by Mariano Fortuny casts a forbidding light. The brushed stainless-steel panels – sculptures by Japanese-American artist Jerry Kamitaki – add to the disturbing atmosphere.*

*Left: The bare, ascetic metal chairs that surround the table in the office were designed by the Comme des Garçons studio.*

## LIFE OF A POET

With his portrait by the American photographer Richard Avedon, his paintings by his friend Kuniyoshi Kaneko, and his shoes by the fashion designer Tokio Kumagai, Mutsuro Takahashi, one of Japan's modern poets, has succeeded in integrating Western and Oriental themes in the old house where he has lived for 15 years. Set among tall trees on a quiet street in the Setagaya section of Tokyo, the unusually old Western-style wooden house was built in 1933.

Takahashi works in the spacious book-lined second-floor room surrounded by some of his favorite art. Downstairs, in the atmospheric small sitting room, are accumulated his souvenirs—antique dolls and eyeglasses, sword handles and figurines, photographs and prints.

*Left:* A spider weaves a web outside Mutsuro Takahashi's suburban house.

*Above Right:* Over the front door hangs a photographic portrait of the poet.

*Above Center Right:* An old-fashioned telephone sits on a small chest in an alcove on the ground floor.

*Above Far Right:* German Boy is the name of the 1971 glass-enclosed sculpture by Simon Yotsuya in the entrance hall.

*Right:* The cluttered sitting room on the ground floor is the repository for the poet's memorabilia. The oil painting is by Kuniyoshi Kaneko.

*Right:* Only a few blocks away from the fashion-conscious Shibuya shopping area, the Pink Dragon looks as if it has just flown in from California or South Miami Beach. Pink, beige, and tropical, the building includes a nightclub and cafe, a street-level shop, and on the top floor a pied-à-terre for the owner.

**Above:** *A pair of chrome-and-leather waiting room armchairs from the 1930s are positioned in Masayuki Yamazaki's apartment.*

**Right:** *In the open kitchen the work counter is black-tiled. Pink and white checked tiles cover two of the walls.*

**Right:** *The glamorous leopard-patterned sofa and the artist's palette-shaped table date from the 1950s.*

***Above:*** *A dinette table with matching chrome chairs is set with American Fiestaware.*

***Left:*** *Black and white checked tiles completely cover every surface in the bathroom and surround the lilac-colored tub.*

***Above and Right:*** *Instead of palm trees, the rooftop swimming pool has a view of central Tokyo.*

## RECORD COLLECTIONS

Hiroshi Nagai – an illustrator, passionate collector of rhythm and blues records, and fan of American Pop culture – lives in a small apartment in one of Tokyo's most architecturally avant-garde structures. The apartment house dates from the 1960s, when the city was rebuilding itself.

Nagai decided to take down all of the apartment's interior walls, but retained the extraordinary futuristic stainless-steel kitchen unit. That he likes having objects in multiples is obvious from the minute one enters the apartment. Dozens of pairs of sneakers, 10,000 45-rpm records, and over 7,000 long-playing records are both a collector's prizes and an essential part of the decor.

*Top Far Left, Top Left, and Above Left: The 1960s building was considered avant-garde in its time. The entrance is at the bottom of a wide stairway, and the guardian's lodge is a study in kitsch.*

*Above: Hiroshi Nagai's thousands of records are neatly lined up in a gridlike wall of cubicles, or stored in boxes on the floor.*

*Right: The graphic designer's clothes hang from exposed pipes above his work area.*

**Left:** *The stainless-steel kitchen is now accessorized with a working soda machine and jukebox.*

**Below Left:** *The seating area is furnished with a Le Corbusier sofa and armchairs.*

*Right: The windows at the end of the room are covered with traditional Japanese shoji screens. The chaise is by Le Corbusier.*

*Below Right: Stacks of videotapes are stored under the kitchen counter. The chrome metal-weave chairs are by the American designer Harry Bertoia.*

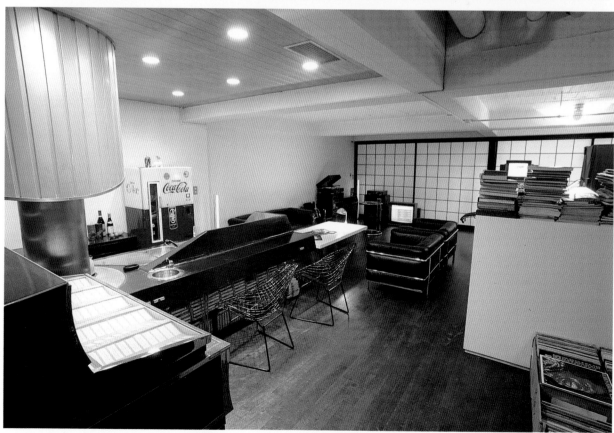

## MONUMENTAL SCALE

Kumihiko and Chihaya Nakagawas' recently completed house in the Kasuya suburb of Tokyo is at once a living place, an artist's studio, and a private art gallery. He is a famous movie director and screenwriter in the circle of Alain Robbe-Grillet, the avant-garde French writer; she is a sculptor who works with textiles, creating monumental pieces, often for public spaces.

Jiro Murofushi was the architect of the house, which was built on a limited budget, using industrial materials such as concrete, galvanized aluminum, and corrugated iron. One of the building's unusual features is a series of platforms that can be adjusted to different heights, adding extra flexibility to the interior spaces.

*Above Left: Kumihiko Nakagawa sits in his second-floor office.*

*Far Left: A simple arrangement of branches decorates the courtyard.*

*Left: The front door is inset into a metallic-painted wood entrance.*

*Below Left: The roof is a vault of corrugated iron.*

*Right: A large steel and silk sculpture by Chihaya Nakagawa is suspended at the far end of the living space, which also functions as a gallery.*

**Left:** The spools of thread used by Chihaya Nakagawa for her textile pieces have a sculptural quality.

**Below Left:** The wool carpet in front of the fireplace was created by the sculptor.

**Right and Center Right:** Lightweight galvanized-aluminum construction ladders are set on wheels for maneuverability.

**Far Right:** A movable podiumlike stair bridges the different heights between the entrance and the living area.

**Below Right:** Above the fireplace, a tiny television screen is part of an aluminum sculpture.

**Below Center Right:** Chihaya Nakagawa took advantage of the holes in the concrete structure to anchor one of her textile pieces.

**Below Far Right:** An electronically controlled car sits in the gallery.

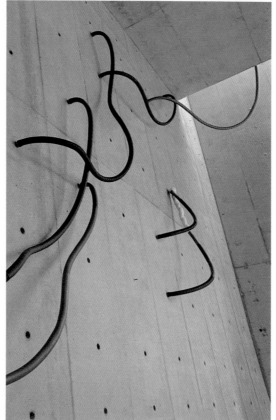

**Above:** *One wall of the bathroom, with its panoply of electric switches, is reminiscent of a space ship control board. In contrast, the shower curtain hangs from a ceiling rod around the old-fashioned bathtub. A washing machine is located under a granite counter.*

**Left:** *A narrow stair leads from the living area to the bathroom.*

*Above and Right:* The domed corrugated-iron ceiling encloses Kumihiko Nakagawa's office. A wide platform and storage unit near the window doubles as an extra sleeping area.

## STREET FARE

Few sights exemplify the frenetic pace of life and business in Tokyo as much as the colorful vending machines that sprout up on a daily basis along the streets of the city. The units add an extra element of visual variety to the urban scene.

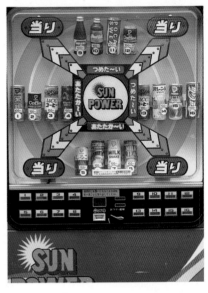

*Above and Left:* Brightly patterned vending machines are ubiquitous on Japanese city streets and offer such items as batteries, ice cream, soft drinks, iced coffee, liquor, and magazines.

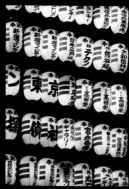

# CATALOGUE OF SOURCES

From whole rooms, complete with tatami mat-covered floors and sliding shoji screen partitions, to decorative accessories such as lacquer trays and ceramic bowls, the Japanese look has long been popular in this country. While most Japanese imports for the home were once categorized as crafts or electronics, in the last few years there has been a wider diversity of items available. Along with modern ceramics, contemporary Japanese furniture is becoming better known in the United States. In many cities Japanese shops feature a large selection of inexpensive furnishings, while more specialized antiques dealers offer rarer objects. Large department stores may also carry a broad range of wares from Japan. In the catalogue we have keyed sources to the symbols: R for Retailer, W for Wholesaler, and MO for Mail Order. Listings for museum collections of Japanese art and Japanese gardens open to the public are also included.

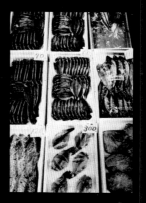

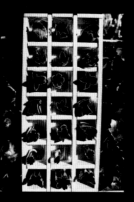

# ANTIQUES

**ALBERTS – LANGDON, INC.**
126 Charles St.
Boston, MA 02114
(617) 523-5954

*Porcelains, paintings, and furniture. (R)*

**ART ASIA, INC.**
1086 Madison Ave.
New York, NY 10028
(212) 249-7250

*Porcelains, lacquerwares, baskets, furniture, and wood-block prints. Vintage kimonos, obis. (R)*

**ASAKICHI**
Japan Center, West Building
1730 Geary Blvd.
San Francisco, CA 94115
(415) 921-2147

*A wide variety of tansu chests, writing boxes, antique Imari porcelain, new pottery and tableware, antique cotton fabrics, and folding bamboo screens. (R)*

**ASIAN ART CENTER**
2647 Connecticut Ave. NW
Washington, DC 20008
(202) 234-3333

*Screens, scrolls, lacquerware, and porcelains. (R)*

**AZUMA GALLERY**
50 Walker St.
New York, NY 10013
(212) 925-1381

*Ceramics, sculptures, prints. (R)*

**BERNHEIMER'S ANTIQUE ARTS**
52C Brattle St.
Cambridge, MA 02138
(617) 547-1177

*Porcelains, prints, scrolls, screens, and textiles. (R)*

**CHARLES DAVID LTD.**
Manhattan Art and Antiques Center
1050 Second Ave., #50A
New York, NY 10022
(212) 688-2210

*Antiques of the Edo and Meiji periods; lacquers, bronzes, netsuke, inro, tsuba, and porcelains. (R) (W)*

**THE CRANE & TURTLE**
2550 California St.
San Francisco, CA 94115
(415) 567-7383

*Antique and contemporary Japanese furnishings and folk art – ceramics, baskets, tansu, screens, scrolls, lacquer, and folk toys. Also traditional Japanese crafts by Japanese-American producers. (R)*

**DIANE GENRE**
603 Julia St.
New Orleans, LA 70130
(504) 525-7270

*Ceramics, bronzes, screens, cloisonné, furniture, textiles, statuary, lacquer, baskets, and bamboo carvings. Also a fine selection of wood-block prints. (R)*

**DYNASTY ANTIQUES AND GIFTS**
3100 Kingman St.
Clearview Plaza
Metairie, LA 70004
(504) 885-2680

*Tansu chests, prints, scrolls, porcelain, and antique obis. (R)*

**EAST & ORIENT COMPANY**
2901 North Henderson
Dallas, TX 75206
(214) 826-1191

*Screens, porcelains, lacquer-wares, and sculpture. (R) (W)*

**EAST EAST, INC.**
230 East 80th St.
New York, NY 10028
(212) 861-3692

*Antique Oriental textiles, including a large selection of kimonos and obis. (R)*

**FAR EASTERN ANTIQUES, INC.**
799 Broadway
New York, NY 10003
(212) 460-5030

*Chests and other furniture. Screens, porcelains, ceramics, and decorative accessories from the 18th to the 20th century. (W)*

**FLYING CRANES ANTIQUES**
Manhattan Art and Antiques Center
1050 Second Ave., Gallery 94
New York, NY 10022
(212) 223-4600

*Porcelains, Satsuma, cloisonné, bronzes, ivories, silver, lacquer screens, paintings from the 18th and 19th centuries. (R) (W) (MO)*

**FUMIKI FINE ARTS**
1894 Union St.
San Francisco, CA 94123
(415) 922-0573

*Tansu chests, netsuke, porcelains, and obis. (R) (MO)*

**THE GALERIE**
122 Middlesex Pike, Rte. 154
Chester, CT 06412
(203) 526-2967
(Call for appointment.)

*Porcelains, prints, suiteki. (R) (W)*

**GARRICK C. STEPHENSON**
50 East 57th St., 7th floor
New York, NY 10022
(212) 753-2570

*Eighteenth- to early 19th-century Japanese lacquer furniture; 19th-century Japanese vases. (R) (W)*

**GORDON FOSTER**
1322 Third Ave.
New York, NY 10021
(212) 744-4922

*Tansu chests and ceramics. Contemporary mingei and baskets. (R) (W) (MO)*

**GRACIE**
879 Third Ave.
New York, NY 10022
(212) 753-5350

*Furniture, porcelain vases, and Japanese screens. Also wallpapers. (W)*

**GUMP'S**
The Galleria, Suite 1105
13350 Dallas Parkway
Dallas, TX 75240
(214) 392-0200

*Screens, antique furnishings, prints, garden stools, and lanterns. (R)*

**LIZA HYDE**
by appointment: (212) 752-3581

*Specializing in fine quality antique screens and kimonos. (R)*

**KUROMATSU**
722 Bay St.
San Francisco, CA 94109
(415) 474-4027

*Edo period pottery and fabrics, ceramics, wood carvings, Japanese chests, old baskets, mingei, and decorative accessories. (R) (W)*

**J. J. LALLY & CO. ORIENTAL ART**
42 East 57th St.
New York, NY 10022
(212) 371-3380

Selection of early Japanese art; ceramics, screens, sculptures, and lacquerwares. (R)

LOYD-PAXTON, INC.
3636 Maple Ave.
Dallas, TX 75219
(214) 521-1521

Period screens, textiles, and tapestries, porcelains, lacquerwares, cloisonné, garden items, and robes. (R) (W)

LORIN MARSH LTD.
979 Third Ave.
New York, NY 10022
(212) 759-8700

Furniture, altar tables, tansu, porcelains, screens, dolls, lacquerware, hibachi tables, and decorative accessories. (W)

MICHAEL B. WEISBROD
987 Madison Ave.
New York, NY 10021
(212) 734-6350

Ceramics and bronzes. (R)

MICHIKO'S GIFTS AND ART
1841 Solano Ave.
Berkeley, CA 94707
(415) 525-2707

Screens, scrolls, porcelains, prints, and furnishings. (R)

NAGA ANTIQUES LTD.
145 East 61st St.
New York, NY 10021
(212) 593-2788

Screens, sculpture, ceramics, furniture, and lacquer. (R) (W)

ORIENTAL PORCELAIN GALLERY
2702 Hyde St.
San Francisco, CA 94109
(415) 776-5969

Nineteenth-century porcelains, mostly Imari, and selected modern ceramics. (R)

ORIENTALIA
1774 Solano Ave.
Berkeley, CA 94707
(415) 526-2210

Tansu chests, porcelains, baskets, screens, and decorative accessories. (R)

ORIENTATIONS
34 Maiden Lane
San Francisco, CA 94108
(415) 981-3972

Tansu chests, screens and paintings, pottery vessels, bronzes and baskets, Imari and other porcelains. (R)

RISING SUN GALLERY
2410 Rice Blvd.
Houston, TX 77005
(713) 521-2322

Screens, scrolls, porcelains, ceramics, antique furniture, tansu, and lacquers. (R)

RUDI SOUTH, INC.
1519C Highline
Dallas, TX 75207
(214) 742-6921

Sculpture, screens, scrolls, ceramics, and textiles. (W)

SHINBI CORP.
55 Greenwich Ave.
New York, NY 10014
(212) 924-2234

Antique and new kimonos, fabrics, and accessories. (R)

SUGIMOTO WORKS OF ART
398 West Broadway
New York, NY 10012
(212) 431-6176

Ceramics, paintings, sculptures, tansu, and antique Japanese folk art and furniture. (R)

TAKAHASHI
215 15th St.
San Francisco, CA 94103
(415) 431-8300

Tansu chests, screens, obis, and furniture. (R)

TANIA CHEN COLLECTIONS, INC.
944 Madison Ave.
New York, NY 10021
(212) 650-0207

Porcelain, paintings, and furniture. (R)

THINGS JAPANESE
1109 Lexington Ave.
New York, NY 10021
(212) 249-3591

Imari porcelains, prints, furniture, baskets, mingei, scrolls, kimonos, and obis. (R) (W)

YUZEN LTD.
318 East 6th St.
New York, NY 10003
(212) 677-0791
429 Caroline St.
Key West, FL 33040
(305) 294-4323

Kimonos of the 19th and 20th centuries. (R)

## BONSAI PLANTS AND GARDEN SUPPLIES

BONSAI BY DEBBIE
1404 Deer Run
Gurnee, IL 60031
(312) 336-8519

Trees, pots, and tools. (R) (W) (MO)

BONSAI DESIGNS
1862 Newbridge Rd.
North Bellmore, NY 11710
(516) 785-1330
Showroom at:
855 Lexington Ave.
New York, NY 10021

Plants, planters, stone lanterns, and rocks. Sold in major East Coast malls on seasonal basis. Call for locations. (R) (W) (MO)

BONSAI DYNASTY CO., INC.
851 Sixth Ave.
New York, NY 10001
(212) 695-2973

Plants, related tools, supplies; rare plants, cacti, succulents. (R) (W)

BONSAI WEST
213 Washington St.
Brookline, MA 02146
(617) 738-7388

Trees, pots, and tools. Private collections available by appointment. (R) (W)

THE GARDEN SOURCE LTD.
4096 Clairmont Rd.
Atlanta, GA 30341
(404) 451-5356

Plants up to 300 years old; antique and new planters, tools, stone and iron lanterns, Ikebana supplies and classes.

GUMP'S
The Galleria, Suite 1105
13350 Dallas Parkway
Dallas, TX 75240
(214) 392-0200

Garden stools, lanterns, and fountains. (R) (MO)

**LOYD-PAXTON, INC.**
3636 Maple Ave.
Dallas, TX 75219
(214) 521-1521

*Antique garden items. (R) (W)*

**ORIENTATIONS**
34 Maiden Lane
San Francisco, CA 94108
(415) 981-3972

*Antique garden lanterns and other fixtures. (R)*

**SHIBUMI TRADING LTD.**
P.O. Box 1-F, Dept. JS1
Eugene, OR 97440
(503) 683-1331 in Oregon
(800) 843-2565 toll-free outside Oregon

*Stone lanterns and basins, bonsai tools and supplies. (W) (MO)*

**SOKO HARDWARE**
1698 Post St.
San Francisco, CA 94115
(415) 931-5510

*Bonsai tools and pots, Ikebana tools and vases, garden decorations. (R)*

**STONE SHADOW LTD.**
799 Widgeon St.
Foster City, CA 94404
(415) 341-1459

*Antique Asian garden art such as stone lanterns, water basins, statuary, and carved antique garden stones. (R) (W)*

**TOGURI MERCANTILE COMPANY**
851 West Belmont Ave.
Chicago, IL 60657
(312) 929-3500

*Bonsai and floral arrangement supplies, garden lanterns. (R) (MO)*

# CONTEMPORARY FURNITURE AND ACCESSORIES

**AKARI ASSOCIATES**
32-37 Vernon Blvd.
Long Island City, NY 11106
(718) 204-7088

Akari
1129 State St., Suite E
Santa Barbara, CA 93101
(805) 966-9557

*Paper lantern lights designed by Isamu Noguchi, made of mulberry bark paper. (R) (W) (MO)*

**ATELIER INTERNATIONAL LTD.**
International Design Center
of New York
30-20 Thomson Avenue
Long Island City, NY 11101
(718) 392-0300

*Furniture designed by Toshiyuki Kita for Cassina. (W)*

**CITY**
213 W. Institute Pl.
Chicago, IL 60610
(312) 664-9581

*Glassware and tabletop accessories. (R)*

**CONTRE-JOUR, INC.**
190 Columbus Ave.
New York, NY 10023
(212) 877-7900

*Japanese flatware, vases, glassware,* kensans, *and Ikebana shears, housewares and gifts, origami cards. (R)*

**D. F. SANDERS & CO.**
386 West Broadway
New York, NY 10012
952 Madison Ave.
New York, NY 10021
(212) 925-9040

*Lamps, table accessories, stationery, and adult toys. (R)*

**EASTERN ACCENT**
237 Newbury St.
Boston, MA 02116
(617) 266-9797

*Tools, frames, and desk accessories by contemporary designers. (R) (W) (MO)*

**FURNITURE OF THE 20TH CENTURY**
227 West 17th St., 2nd floor
New York, NY 10011
(212) 929-6023

*Furniture designed by Comme des Garçons Studio; chairs of welded steel, unfinished or painted black, with grid seat; triangular tables of welded steel with tops of irregularly cut granite. (R) (W)*

**GALLERY 91**
91 Grand St.
New York, NY 10013
(212) 966-3722

*Lighting and home accessories, tableware, stationery, cutlery, and desk accessories by contemporary Japanese designers. Limited editions and traditional crafts. (R)*

**HERMAN MILLER, INC.**
8500 Byron Rd.
Zealand, MI 49464
(800) 642-7944 in Michigan
(800) 851-1196 outside Michigan

*Coffee table designed by Isamu Noguchi, glass top with walnut or ebony base. (W)*

**INDUSTRIAL REVOLUTION**
7560 Melrose Ave.
Los Angeles, CA 90046
(213) 651-2893

*Modern flatware, ceramics, lacquerware, and glasses. Desk accessories, tools, Isamu Noguchi lamps, cast-iron ashtrays, picture frames, and clocks. (R)*

**MODERNAGE**
795 Broadway
New York, NY 10003
(212) 674-5603

**MODERNAGE TEXAS, INC.**
1444 Oaklawn Ave., Suite 590
Dallas, TX 75207
(214) 742-3003

*Lacquered furniture and mirrors by Kazuhide Takahama and Hiroyuki Toyoda. (R) (W)*

**MYTHOLOGY UNLIMITED, INC.**
370 Columbus Ave.
New York, NY 10024
(212) 874-0774

*Robots, wind-up and radio-controlled toys,* chiogami *papers, carved wooden Samurai charms, and framed fabric stencils. (R)*

**NIGHTINGALE'S**
4354 Lovers Lane
Dallas, TX 75225
(214) 368-5460

*Office, bath, and kitchen accessories; Japanese tools. (R)*

**SOINTU**
20 East 69th St.
New York, NY 10021
(212) 570-9449

*Lacquerware, porcelain, and cast iron as well as unusual designs in rubber, plastics, and metals. (R)*

**XENLIGHT**
2311 Prince St.
Berkeley, CA 94705
(415) 549-2857

*Wall, hanging, and table lighting fixtures designed by Hisa Ishikawa. (R) (W) (MO)*

## HANDCRAFTS

ASAKICHI
Japan Center, West Building
1730 Geary Blvd.
San Francisco, CA 94115
(415) 921-2147

*New art porcelains and tableware from kilns in Arita and Kyushu. (R)*

ASIAPHILE
7975 Melrose Ave.
Los Angeles, CA 90046
(213) 653-4744

*Contemporary crafts. (R)*

AZUMA GALLERY
50 Walker St.
New York, NY 10013
(212) 925-1381

*Japanese-style contemporary ceramics. (R)*

GORDON FOSTER
1322 Third Ave.
New York, NY 10021
(212) 744-4922

*Contemporary baskets, ceramics, and cast-iron works. (R) (W) (MO)*

JAPONESQUE
50 Post St.
Crocker Center Galleria, 54
San Francisco, CA 94116
(415) 938-8577

*Fine arts, original paintings, sculpture, ceramics, glass, lacquer, and wood crafts. Contemporary prints. (R)*

KIKU SUI GALLERY
101 Charles St.
Boston, MA 02114
(617) 227-4288

*Handcrafted items including ceramics, mingei, lacquerwares, and kimonos. (R) (W)*

MASHIKO FOLKCRAFT
Japan Center, West Building
1581 Webster St.
San Francisco, CA 94115
(415) 346-0746

*One-of-a-kind pottery from Japanese kilns, including Bizen, Raku, Seto, and Mashiko; Kiaki wood items and bark items from Akita. (R)*

SUGIMOTO WORKS OF ART
398 West Broadway
New York, NY 10012
(212) 431-6176

*Antique and contemporary baskets, ceramics, furniture. (R)*

ZONA
97 Greene St.
New York, NY 10012
(212) 925-6750

*Handcrafted pottery, glassware, and wooden boxes. (R) (MO)*

## HOUSEWARES AND GIFTS

ASIAN TREASURES
2050 Stemmons Freeway
World Trade Center, Suite #9058
Dallas, TX 75258
(214) 698-1781

*Porcelain, including fishbowls; lamps, vases, figurines, wall screens, obis, furnishings. (W)*

AZUMA INTERNATIONAL, INC.
251 East 86th St.
New York, NY 10028
(212) 369-4928
(Four other locations in Manhattan)

Azuma Fifth Avenue Plaza, Inc.
West Belt Mall, Rte. 23
Wayne, NJ 07470
(201) 256-6466

*Ceramics, porcelains, tableware, lacquerware, cooking utensils, and gifts. (R)*

DRAGON TRADING CO.
1709 Locust St.
St. Louis, MO 63103
(314) 621-2221

*Kitchenwares, gifts. (R) (W) (MO)*

HORAI-SAN KITCHENWARE SHOP
240 Washington St.
P.O. Box 482
Brookline, MA 02147
(617) 277-7834

*Kitchenware items including cast-iron cooking pots, clay and ceramic pots; wooden utensils, china, tea sets, sake sets. (R) (MO)*

INTERNATIONAL TRADING CO.
340 East Azusa St.
Los Angeles, CA 90012
(213) 628-7473

*Decorative vases, plates, porcelains, and earthenwares; bronze vases and figurines; zinc and iron accessories; noren room-divider curtains, ykata robes. (R)*

KATAGIRI & CO., INC.
224 East 59th St.
New York, NY 10022
(212) 755-3566

*Chinaware, lacquerware, and food utensils. (R) (M)*

KIYO'S, INC.
2831 N. Clark St.
Chicago, IL 60657
(312) 935-0619

*Porcelains and earthenwares; traditional tableware, tea sets, sake sets; kimonos, obis, and accessories; Ikebana vases, kenzan, go games. (R)*

ORIENTAL ARTS
530 Westbury Square
Houston, TX 77035
(713) 723-7536

*Porcelain, Imari, kimonos, dolls. (R)*

SHIBUMI TRADING LTD.
P.O. Box 1-F, Dept JS1
Eugene, OR 97440
(503) 683-1331 in Oregon
(800) 843-2565 toll-free outside Oregon

*Vases, clothes, tableware, calligraphy sets, tea-ceremony sets, sake sets, sushi presses, dolls, kimonos. (W) (MO)*

SOKO HARDWARE
1698 Post St.
San Francisco, CA 94115
(415) 931-5510

*Cookware, cutlery, tansu hardware, furo. Woodworking hand tools. (R)*

TOGURI MERCANTILE COMPANY
851 W. Belmont Ave.
Chicago, IL 60657
(312) 929-3500

*Lacquerware, tableware, dry goods, kitchenware, woks, home furnishings. (R) (MO)*

## PRINTS

ASIAPHILE
7975 Melrose Ave.
Los Angeles, CA 90046
(213) 653-4744

*Nineteenth-century prints and Japanese photographs. (R)*

DIANE GENRE
603 Julia St.
New Orleans, LA 70130
(504) 525-7270
*Fine quality wood-block prints of the 18th and 19th centuries. (R)*

GLASS GALLERY
315 Central Park West, Apt. 8W
New York, NY 10024
(212) 787-4704
*Ukiyoe prints. (R)*

INTERNATIONAL ART GUILD
GALLERY
Japan Center
1581 Webster St.
San Francisco, CA 94115
(415) 567-4390
*Japanese wood-block prints from the 18th to the 20th century. (R)(W)*

JAPAN GALLERY
1210 Lexington Ave.
New York, NY 10028
(212) 288-2241
*Prints. (R)*

KIKU SUI GALLERY
101 Charles St.
Boston, MA 02114
(617) 227-4288
*Antique and modern Japanese wood-block prints. (R)(W)(MO)*

KIMURA GALLERY & FRAMING
1933 Ocean Ave.
San Francisco, CA 94127-2795
(415) 585-0052
482 Hamilton Ave.
Palo Alto, CA 94301
(415) 322-3984
*Wood-block prints from the 18th to the 20th century; contemporary prints; scrolls dating from the 1660s; antique chests; folk art. (R)(W)*

MARY BASKETT GALLERY
1002 St. Gregory St.
Cincinnati, OH 45202
(513) 421-0460
*Contemporary Japanese art; paintings, prints, and screens. Ceramics and glass. (R)(W)(MO)*

RICHARD REED ARMSTRONG
FINE ART
1446 N Dearborn
Chicago, IL 60610
(312) 664-9312 (by appointment)
*Ukiyoe wood-block prints from the 18th, 19th, and early 20th century. (R)*

RISING SUN GALLERY
2410 Rice Blvd.
Houston, TX 77005
(713) 521-2322
*Ukiyoe and contemporary limited editions prints; wood-block, silk-screen prints; screens, scrolls. (R)*

RONIN GALLERY
605 Madison Ave.
New York, NY 10022
(212) 688-0188
*Extensive collection of 17th- to 20th-century wood-block prints; also paintings, pottery, netsuke, and tsuba. (R)(W)(MO)*

THINGS JAPANESE
1109 Lexington Ave.
New York, NY 10021
(212) 249-3591
*Prints. (R)(W)*

## TRADITIONAL JAPANESE FURNISHINGS

ARISE FUTON MATTRESS
CO., INC.
57 Greene St.
New York, NY 10013
(212) 925-0310
Call for addresses for other locations in New York City.

65 Tarrytown Rd.
White Plains, NY 10607
(914) 946-8740
*Futons, pillows, bolsters, and bed frames. (R)(MO)*

ASIAN HOUSE OF CHICAGO
316 N. Michigan Ave.
Chicago, IL 60601
(312) 782-9577
*Screens, lamps, furnishings. (R)(W)*

AZUMA INTERNATIONAL, INC.
251 East 86th St.
New York, NY 10028
(212) 369-4928
(Four other locations in Manhattan)

Azuma Fifth Avenue Plaza, Inc.
West Belt Mall, Rte. 23
Wayne, NJ 07470
(201) 256-6466
*Shoji screens and lamps, futons, bed frames, pillows, screens, furniture, rice-paper shades, and home accessories. (R)*

BLUE HORIZONS
205 Florida St.
San Francisco, CA 94103
(415) 626-1602
*Shoji screens, tatami mats, and lamps. Custom screens and Oriental furnishings. (R)(MO)*

CONRAN'S
160 East 54th St.
New York, NY 10022
(212) 371-2225
(Stores also in Fairfax, VA; Georgetown, Washington, DC; Hackensack, NJ; King of Prussia, PA; Manhasset and New Rochelle, NY; and Willow Grove, PA)
Mail order only:
145 Huguenot St.
New Rochelle, NY 10801
(914) 632-0515 in New York
(800) 431-2718 outside New York
*Futon beds; "Tokyo" lamp. (R)(MO)*

CRATE & BARREL
1045 Massachusetts Ave.
Cambridge, MA 02138
(617) 547-3994
*Futons and bed frames. (R)*

EURO 2000/ESCAPADES
800 N. Clark
Chicago, IL 60610
(312) 664-7766
*Futons, furniture, lamps, and accessories. (R)*

FIVE EGGS
436 West Broadway
New York, NY 10012
(212) 226-1606
*Futons, lamps, tatami mats, roll-up shades. Traditional clothing including kimonos, yukata, and socks. Vases and tools for Ikebana. Folk items, origami, cookware. (R)(MO)*

FUJI GROUP OF AMERICA, INC.
Design Center of Los Angeles
433 South Spring St., Suite 5C
Los Angeles, CA 90013
(213) 621-2703

*Authentic Japanese tatami and tea-ceremony rooms in prefabricated units to be adapted to existing rooms, entryways, patios, or gardens, and assembled on site in a few hours. Can be individually tailored with choice of colors, sizes, accessories. (R) (W)*
Can also be seen at:
Sino-American Furniture Center
27-33 West 23rd St.
New York, NY 10010
(212) 741-8833

FUTON FURNISHINGS
607 W. Belmont
Chicago, IL 60657
(312) 883-0040
809 N. Dempster
Evanston, IL 60201
(312) 864-1002

*Futons and bed frames, pillows, shoji screens, and lamps. (R)*

THE FUTON SHOP
491 Broadway
New York, NY 10012
(212) 226-5825

*Futons, tatami mats, and cotton quilts. (R) (W)*

GRACIE
979 Third Ave.
New York, NY 10022
(212) 753-5350

*Hand-painted wallpapers and textured wall coverings, including grass cloths and silks. (W)*

GRILLION CORPORATION
189-193 First St.
Brooklyn, NY 11215
(718) 875-8545

*Custom shoji screens, dividers, and wall panels in lacquered mahogany. (R) (W)*

JAPANESE SCREEN
23-37 91st St.
East Elmhurst, NY 11369
(718) 803-2267

*Custom shoji screens, tatami mats, fusuma doors, tearooms, platform beds, lights. (R) (W) (MO)*

THE JAPAN TRADING CO.
1762 Buchanan St.
San Francisco, CA 94115
(415) 929-0989

*Shoji screens, tatami mats, fusuma doors, furnishings, and custom-made Japanese rooms and alcoves. (R) (MO)*

KIYOTO DESIGN INSTITUTE
7485 West 151st St.
Stanley, KA 66223
(913) 897-2366

*Authentic Japanese house filled with shoji screens, lighting fixtures, handmade furniture, paintings, prints, and pottery for sale. Custom interiors and accessories available. (R) (MO)*

JACK LENOR LARSEN
41 East 11th St.
New York, NY 10003
(212) 674-3993

*Fabrics and wall coverings. (W)*

L.A. SHOJI & DECORATIVE PRODUCTS
4844-48 W. Jefferson
Los Angeles, CA 90016
(213) 732-9161

*Shoji screens, sliding doors, room dividers, fusuma doors, MOOM bridges, toriis. (R) (W) (MO)*

MIKADO (J. C. TRADING, INC.)
Japan Center, Nos. 8, 9, 10
1737 Post St.
San Francisco, CA 94115-3698
(415) 922-9450

*Futons, tatami mats, tea-ceremony equipment, Japanese-style dishes, and toys. (R) (MO)*

MIYA SHOJI & INTERIORS, INC.
107 West 17th St.
New York, NY 10011
(212) 243-6774

*Custom shoji screens, fusuma screens, Japanese rooms, cabinets, light fixtures, and stone lanterns. (R) (W) (MO)*

NATURAL DESIGN
1801 W. Larchmont
Chicago, IL 60613
(312) 327-6800

*Futons, tatami mats, shoji screens and lamps, pillows, bed frames, tatami and tori tables. (R) (W) (MO)*

NEW MOON
1393 Beacon St.
Brookline, MA 02146
(617) 566-1431
1030 Massachusetts Ave.
Cambridge, MA 02139
(617) 492-8262

*Futons and frames, shoji screens, tatami mats, accessories. (R) (W) (MO)*

NOH MASK
285 Bellevue Square
Bellevue, WA 98004
(206) 455-9773

*Futons and frames, vintage kimonos. (R) (W)*

NORTHWEST FUTON COMPANY
400 SW Second Ave.
Portland, OR 97204
(503) 242-0057
516 East 15th Ave.
East Seattle, WA 98112
(206) 323-0936

*Futons and frames, furniture and lighting, tatami mats, shoji screens, cushions, and accessories. Kimonos and yukatas. (R) (W) (MO)*

CHARLES D. WALKER MFG. CO.
1237 Minnesota St.
San Francisco, CA 94107
(415) 285-7111

*Custom-made shoji screens. (R)*

SANCTUARY FUTON CO.
217 Church St.
Philadelphia, PA 19106
(215) 925-9460

*Futons, bed frames, tatami mats, and pillows. (R)*

TAKAHASHI
668 Bridgeway
Sausalito, CA 94965
(415) 332-2668
Mail order:
235 15th St.
San Francisco, CA 94103
(415) 431-8300

*Shoji panels, painted screens, tatami mats, bath accessories. (R)*

TANSUYA CORPORATION
159 Mercer St.
New York, NY 10012
(212) 966-1782

*Custom Japanese lacquer furniture and screens. Hand-printed paper products. (R) (W) (MO)*

TOGE WOODWORKING & DESIGN
Hunter's Point Shipyard
P.O. Box 882452
San Francisco, CA 94188
(415) 771-4438

*Electrified reproductions of maru-andon lamps made of lacquered cedarwood and mulberry paper. (R) (W)*

UWAJIMAYA, INC.
6th Ave. S. & S. King St.
Seattle, WA 98104
(206) 624-6248
15555 NE. 24th St.
Bellevue, WA 98007
(206) 747-9012
Southern Mall
Tukwila, WA 98188
(206) 246-7077

*Futons and furnishings, wooden bath accessories. (R) (W) (MO)*

# MUSEUM COLLECTIONS

It is advisable to call in advance for days and times of opening.

ALLEN MEMORIAL ART MUSEUM
Oberlin College
Main and Lorrain Sts.
Oberlin, OH 44074
(216) 775-8665

*The Ainsworth collection of over 1,500 prints. Available for viewing by appointment.*

ART INSTITUTE OF CHICAGO
Michigan Ave. & Adams St.
Chicago, IL 60603
(312) 443-3600

*Largest and most complete collection of wood-block prints in the United States. Also screens, and Buddhist sculpture and ceramics. Gift shop sells books, reproductions, and original decorative items.*

ARTHUR M. SACKLER GALLERY
Smithsonian Institution
Independence Ave. at 11th St. SW
Washington, DC 20560

*A new Smithsonian museum specializing in the arts of Asia, including 1,000 objects donated by*

*Dr. Arthur M. Sackler. Shares a gallery shop with the Freer Gallery of Art providing books, cards, reproductions, and slides.*

ARTHUR M. SACKLER MUSEUM
Harvard University Art Museums
485 Broadway
Cambridge, MA 02141
(617) 495-2397

*Japanese prints, paintings, sculpture, textiles, and decorative arts of all periods. Books and cards available.*

ASIA SOCIETY
725 Park Ave.
New York, NY 10021
(212) 288-6400

*Rotating exhibitions from The Mr. and Mrs. John D. Rockefeller III Collection of Asian Art, which includes Japanese paintings, screens, lacquers, and ceramics. Gift shop sells porcelains, ceramics, textiles, wooden toys, and rice papers.*

ASIAN ART MUSEUM OF SAN FRANCISCO
Avery Brundage Collection
Golden Gate Park
San Francisco, CA 94118-4598
(415) 668-8921

*Sculptures, mainly Buddhist; paintings, including hanging scrolls, screens, and hand scrolls; ceramics, lacquers, metalwork, textiles, and armor.*

BOSTON CHILDREN'S MUSEUM
300 Congress St.
Boston, MA 02110
(617) 426-6500

*An authentic Japanese silk weaver's house, shop, garden, and street from Kyoto, furnished for*

*contemporary family life. Study storage area houses 1,500 objects from everyday life. Educational kits for rent. Bookshop sells toys, books, origami papers, and masks.*

THE BROOKLYN MUSEUM
200 Eastern Parkway
Brooklyn, NY 11238
(718) 638-5000

*Collection includes paintings, scrolls, ceramics, costumes, prints, lacquerwares, arms and armor, and mingei art. Gift shop sells antique ceramics, textiles, and objects.*

CLEVELAND MUSEUM OF ART
11150 East Blvd.
Cleveland, OH 44106
(216) 421-7340

*Japanese paintings from Heian to Edo periods; wood and metal sculptures, Kamakura Buddhist and Shinto deities. Ukiyoe prints and paintings; ceramics; lacquers and tea-ceremony utensils. Bookstore sells cards, reproductions, and books.*

CRAFT AND FOLK ART MUSEUM
5814 Wilshire Blvd.
Los Angeles, CA 90036
(213) 937-5544

*Japanese folk art. Books and objects for sale in the gift shop.*

FREER GALLERY OF ART
Smithsonian Institution
Jefferson Drive at 12th St. SW
Washington, DC 20560
(202) 357-2104

*Ceramics, lacquerware, paintings, screens, metalware, and sculpture. Bookshop sells cards,*

*posters, reproductions, slides, and photographs.*

GEORGE WALTER VINCENT SMITH ART MUSEUM
222 State St.
Springfield, MA 01103
(413) 733-4214

*Decorative arts including porcelains, lacquerware, furniture, bronzes, netsuke, and arms and armor. Japanese prints and paintings are available in the adjacent Museum of Fine Arts.*

ISAMU NOGUCHI GARDEN MUSEUM
32-37 Vernon Blvd.
Long Island City, NY 11106
(718) 204-7088

*Sculptures in stone, metal, wood, and paper by Isamu Noguchi as well as models and drawings of his garden and plaza projects. Books and catalogues available; Noguchi's Akari light sculptures for sale. Open from spring to fall only.*

JAPAN HOUSE GALLERY
333 East 47th St.
New York, NY 10017
(212) 832-1155

*Loan exhibitions of Japanese arts.*

KIMBELL ART MUSEUM
3333 Camp Bowie Blvd.
P.O. Box 9440
Fort Worth, TX 76107
(817) 332-8451

*Ceramics, Buddhist paintings and sculptures, lacquers, screens, and scroll paintings.*

LOS ANGELES COUNTY
MUSEUM OF ART
5905 Wilshire Blvd.
Los Angeles, CA 90036
(213) 857-6111

*Japanese paintings, sculpture, and ceramics.*

METROPOLITAN MUSEUM
OF ART
Fifth Ave. at 82nd St.
New York, NY 10028
(212) 879-5500

*Japanese art from 3000 B.C. to late 19th century including Shinto and Buddhist paintings and sculpture, as well as secular paintings, ceramics, lacquers, prints, and textiles. Replicated ceiling and central altar from 12th-century temple and a ceiling designed after the palace interiors. Bookshop offers cards, books, posters, and reproductions of netsuke and ceramics.*

MOUNT HOLYOKE COLLEGE
ART MUSEUM
South Hadley, MA 01075
(413) 538-2245

*Changing exhibitions from the permanent collection of Japanese paintings, prints, ceramics, sculpture, and lacquerware. Postcards available.*

MUSEUM OF ART
Rhode Island School of Design
224 Benefit St.
Providence, RI 02903
(401) 331-3511

*Wood-block prints, including* kachoe *genre prints and* surimono *prints. Important group of Japanese costumes, especially No theater robes. Also paintings, sculpture, and decorative arts.*

*Bookshop sells cards and reproductions of some items.*

MUSEUM OF FINE ARTS
465 Huntington Ave.
Boston, MA 02115
(617) 267-9300

*Japanese paintings and prints; Buddhist sculptures and fine decorative arts. Gift shop sells reproductions of museum items, books, and papers.*

NELSON-ATKINS MUSEUM
OF ART
4525 Oak St.
Kansas City, MO 64111
(816) 561-4000

*Screen paintings, hanging scrolls, ceramics, porcelains, sculpture, and lacquerware. Books available.*

PACIFIC ASIA MUSEUM
46 N. Los Robles Ave.
Pasadena, CA 91101
(818) 449-2742

*Wood-block prints, netsuke, dolls, lacquerware, and textiles.*

PEABODY MUSEUM OF SALEM
East India Square
Salem, MA 01970
(617) 745-1876

*Ethnographic objects from Japan, including tools, lamps, clothing, kitchen equipment, and important collection of glass lantern slides showing daily life in Japan in the 1800s. Gift shop sells antique objects, textiles, photographs, and books.*

SPENCER MUSEUM OF ART
University of Kansas
Lawrence, KA 66045
(913) 864-4710

*Paintings of the Edo period,*

*especially Nanga school. Some Buddhist art, netsuke, and decorative arts. A* tokonoma *is built in the gallery using traditional materials and methods. Books, posters, and cards available.*

THE ST. LOUIS ART MUSEUM
Forest Park
St. Louis, MO 63110
(314) 721-0067

*Bronzes, prints, ceramics, paintings and scrolls.*

THE TEXTILE MUSEUM
2320 S St. NW
Washington, DC 20008
(202) 667-0441

*Collection of Japanese textiles.*

# GARDENS

It is advisable to call in advance for days and times of opening.

ART COMPLEX MUSEUM
189 Alden St.
Duxbury, MA 02331
(617) 934-6634

*Teahouse built in Kyoto and reassembled. Tea garden includes stones, lantern, water basin, steppingstone pathway, and simple plant material.*

BROOKLYN BOTANIC GARDEN
1000 Washington Ave.
Brooklyn, NY 11225
(718) 622-4433

*Japanese hill-and-pond gardens. Extensive collection of bonsai trees, Oriental flowering cherry trees. Japanese Cherry Blossom Festival celebrated first weekend in May. Courses available in bonsai, Ikebana, and* sumie. *Gift shop sells books, tools, and bonsai and Ikebana supplies.*

DENVER BOTANIC GARDENS
909 York St.
Denver, CO 80206
(303) 575-3751

*Garden with bridges, gates, and authentic teahouse. Gift shop.*

GARDEN CENTER OF GREATER
CLEVELAND
11030 East Blvd.
Cleveland, OH 44106
(216) 721-1600

*Garden with stone pagoda. Gift shop.*

MOUNT HOLYOKE COLLEGE
South Hadley, MA 01075
(413) 538-2045

*Meditation garden and teahouse.*

NATIONAL BONSAI
COLLECTION
U.S. National Arboretum
3501 New York Ave. NE
Washington, DC 20002
(202) 475-4858

*Garden complex includes bonsai collection and viewing stones. Many plants and trees from Asia.*

ORIENTAL STROLL GARDEN
The Hammond Museum
Deveau Rd.
North Salem, NY 10560
(914) 669-5135

*Garden of Serenity offers 15 separate Oriental landscapes. Open May through October.*

# INDEX

287

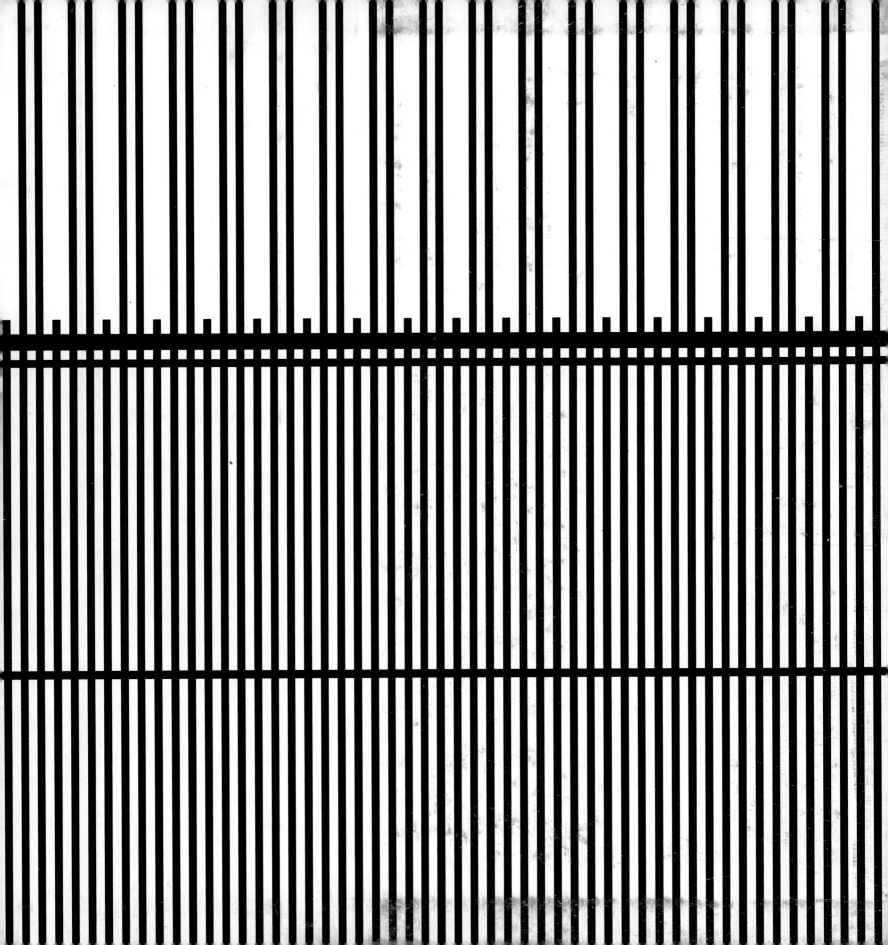